The Crucifixion Code

The truth about why Jesus was crucified and why it became the most impactful event in human history

Ren Lexander

renlexander.com

The Crucifixion Code is part of
The Meaning of Life series:

Stay up to date with releases:

renlexander.com

DEDICATION

Dedicated to Ahrara Bhakti.

Without you, I very much doubt that this book
would exist.

Almost certainly, you will get far more out of reading *The Crucifixion Code*, if you first read *The Jesus Code*.

The Jesus Code explains the real meaning of Jesus' teachings.

Table of Contents

The Enigma of the Cross

Crucifixion is a bad way to die.

A really really bad way to die.

The body slowly tears itself apart under its own weight. The suffering is so agonizing that getting your legs shattered by an iron club is a mercy; having a spear thrust into your side is a kindness; being denied water is a blessing. Such things can hasten an end to your torment.

Your best hope is that the people supervising your agony get bored or have other places they have to be and so intervene with a spear or a club.

With your arms lashed or nailed to the crossbeam, the weight of your body makes it borderline impossible to breathe. You have to hoist yourself up by the strength of your arms to take a shallow breath but that only prolongs the agony. Eventually, the strength of your arms will fail and the weight of your body will strangle you.

It is an exquisite form of torture to put a small platform under your feet or nail your feet to the cross – that enables you to hoist yourself up by the strength of your legs. This may prolong your agony by many hours. Or even days. That is why shattering the bones of the legs is such a kindness. Even better if they shatter the bones of the arms as well.

The body is so comprehensively traumatized by crucifixion that, when death finally comes, it could be occasioned by any number of physical implosions: asphyxiation, cardiac rupture, pulmonary embolism, blood loss, heart failure, sepsis.

It will take many hours to die.

It could take days.

It also involves humiliation.

Before you are hoisted up on the cross, you will be stripped bare. When you urinate, it will run down your legs. If you defecate, it clings to your body, and flies swarm around you. If you live long enough, maggots will breed in your feces and start to worm their way into your body. The stench from your own excrement fills your nostrils.

Even after death, the humiliation continues: your corpse will be left on the cross as a warning to others and carrion birds and rats will tear off your flesh until there are only bones.

The man about to be crucified had already been beaten and bloodied. He had been viciously scourged with a whip made of leather and sharp bones and lead weights. His clothes were already soaked with blood. But even these are ripped from his body.

Nails are driven through his flesh, pinning him to the wood. Then he is hoisted up. As his naked body is jolted into its final place, there comes the first tearing sensation as his body starts to slowly strangle itself.

But there was a very big difference between this particular man and the other men being crucified around him. He had planned to be there. He had entered the seat of power with the specific intent of being arrested and crucified. He had trashed the Temple; he baited the authorities; he slandered them; and, when all this failed, he helped to organize his own arrest. This man had planned this agonizing death for a very particular and peculiar reason: he was certain that this is what God wanted from him.

The priests, whom he had earlier taunted, show up to savor his agony and add to his humiliation. Now it is their turn to make fun of him: "He saved others; he cannot save himself. Let the Messiah, the King of Israel, come down now from the cross that we may see and believe." (Mark 15:31-32)

Even the other criminals being crucified mock him.

But he never responds. No word passes his lips.

The hours pass in excruciating slowness – like the blood dripping, drop by slow drop, from his body. It is only after many hours of this soul-wrenching agony that death starts to mercifully draw near.

As it does, this man's iron-willed control implodes. Words are wrenched from the core of his being. Words so dramatic, so telling, so searingly impactful, that his Greek biographer recorded them in their original Aramaic:

"Eloi, Eloi, lema sabachthani!?"
My God, my God, why have you forsaken me!?

What just happened?
Was this the Son turning on the Father?
Accusing God of deserting him!?
These are this man's final words. The Gospel of Mark records

these as the only words he uttered on the Cross. They are the most enigmatic words in the whole Bible.

They are the Enigma of the Cross.

How did it get to this?

How did it get to a point where an itinerant country preacher colluded in his own arrest and crucifixion?

How did it get to the point where a man who believed he was suffering and dying at the behest of God would, in the last moment of his life, turn on God and scream out the ultimate accusation at his Creator?

The greatest story ever told becomes greater still

Two thousand years ago…

A former construction worker wanders around the backblocks of a third-rate country in the Roman Empire. For, at most, a couple of years, he preaches in obscure parables. He never founds a new religion. He never writes anything down. He has a handful of close disciples - all of whom run away when he is arrested. He dies in ignominious agony nailed to a cross as a criminal.

That should have been the end of that obscure little tale, right?

Two thousand years later…

The posthumous influence of Jesus encircles the globe. History is demarcated from before and after his birth. The religion he followed – Judaism – now has around 14 million followers. The religion founded in his name – Christianity – has around 2.5 billion followers, constituting a third of the human race.

And his influence is still spreading.

Christianity is the fastest-growing minority religion in China. In 1949, there were 4 million Chinese Christians. By 2018, even the Chinese government conceded that the number was 44 million – and that was almost certainly a vast underestimate.

In 1900, there were only nine million Christians in Africa. Currently, the number is 685 million. It is projected that by 2025, there will be 760 million Christians in Africa.[1] In 2010, a Muslim cleric estimated that 16,000 African Muslims are converting to Christianity every day.[2]

---

[1] See the Wikipedia articles "Christianity in Africa" and "Christianity in China".

[2] Sheikh Ahmad Al Katani, the president of The Companions Lighthouse for the Science of Islamic Law in Libya, in a 2010 interview on Al-Jazeerah. See muslimstatistics.wordpress.com/2012/12/14/al-jazeerah-6-million-muslims-convert-to-christianity-in-africa-each-year/.

Even in the West, which is rapidly disappearing into the new Religion of Distractions, the influence of Jesus still looms as inexplicably powerful:

- The 2004 film *The Passion of the Christ* became the largest-grossing non-English-speaking film of all time, taking over $600 million at the box office despite being in Latin and Aramaic and despite most of the film focusing snuff-like on the torture of Jesus.

- In his novel, *The Da Vinci Code*, Dan Brown wove a thriller around the premise that secrets about Jesus's life had been systematically concealed for two thousand years. It became the biggest-selling English-language novel of the 21st Century with 80 million copies sold. The film based on it became the second biggest film of 2006, making $758 million worldwide.

- The 2013 History Channel Series *The Bible* became the biggest-selling mini-series ever in its first week of DVD release, with over half a million copies sold.

- In 2013 alone, there were two number-one best-selling books on Jesus – *Killing Jesus* and *Zealot*.

How could this happen?

How could an obscure Jewish preacher wandering around tiny villages and towns come to dominate the history of the world?

It is, far and away, the most extraordinary story in recorded human history.

And the actual truth about what Jesus taught, why he allowed himself to be crucified, and why Christianity spread and keeps on spreading is a far greater story than has ever previously been told.

We saw in *The Jesus Code* that the historical Jesus was not teaching "worship me as the Son of God, pray, obey the Ten Commandments, and you'll get into the Kingdom of God (heaven) after you die." Jesus was actually the student of a mystic known as John the Baptist. In his time with him, Jesus achieved the pinnacle of the mystic path: Baptism by the Holy Spirit (known in other traditions by names such as "Union with the One", "Union with the Lord of Love" and "Divine Marriage"). And this was the path he taught in the Beatitudes and in his parables.

If this had been the whole story then Jesus would have been swallowed up into the backwaters of history along with John the

Baptist. As Jesus did not write anything down, his thoughts would have been less known to us than, for instance, those of the ancient Indian writers of *The Upanishads*. Jesus was surely destined to join the hidden ranks of anonymous faceless mystics.

Obviously this is not what happened.

Instead, this obscure mystic teaching in a third-rate country of the Roman Empire would become the most famous man in history – the most influential figure in the story of humankind. History would come to be measured before and after his coming: B.C. and A.D.

How could that happen?

It is the most extraordinary thing ever in recorded human history.

As such, the explanation for how this came about was never going to be ordinary. It was always going to be singular and unique. The explanation of it will take us to places where few if any academic historians would dare to tread. It will take us to places where many readers will struggle to go and, like the disciples when Jesus was arrested, some will likely fall away.

To understand the full journey of Jesus, we are going to have to wade even more deeply into our exploration of the spiritual. Many people will get cold and reluctant feet about going this deep. But contemplate this:

> Whatever made you think that you could fully understand a deeply spiritual person such as Jesus without exploring deep spiritual questions?

Right now, billions of people around the globe believe that Jesus was the only begotten Son of God, that his birth was foretold and heralded by angels, that he was born from a virgin, that he walked on water, that he raised the dead, that he died for our sins, that his body came back to life on the third day after his death and that he magically ascended with his corporeal body into a heaven that is otherwise populated only by souls.

Many readers may struggle to wrap their heads around the spiritual drama which will unfold in the course of this book but you will not be challenged to contemplate anything as out-there as stuff like that.

Take a deep breath, gird your loins, and prepare for a dramatic change in the journey of Jesus...

"Are you the one who is to be next?"

As Jesus walks along stony paths preaching in parables, John the Baptist, his teacher, sits in the stony dank dungeon of Herod's prison. John has made peace with the inevitability of his death. Herod imprisoned him to stop him preaching so there is no way that this willful king is ever going to let him out to preach again.

Soon Herod would behead John.

So appalled were the people by this that, when Herod's army later suffered a devastating defeat in a battle against the neighboring army of Aretas of Nabatea, the people said it was God's punishment for Herod imprisoning and executing John the Baptist.[3]

Even Herod's guards and jailors are intimidated by John. They permit some of his disciples to see him.

John is not worried by death. He has confidence that he has evolved his soul and so something better lies on the other side for him. But something else concerns John – something that will happen after his death, something so important that it causes John to send out word to the most senior of his students – the ones who had experienced baptism by the Holy Spirit. He sends out an enigmatic question:

> "Are you the one who is to be next, or shall we look for another?"[4]
>
> - Matthew 11:3

This question is conveyed to Jesus who replies:

> "Go and tell John what you hear and see: the blind receive their sight and the lame walk, lepers are cleansed and the deaf hear, and the dead are raised up, and the poor have good news preached to them. And blessed is the one who is not offended by me."
>
> - Matt 11:4-6

Jesus's reply will be taken back to John in prison. For John, the reply is at least a little disappointing. Instead of giving a direct and clear

---

[3] Josephus, *Antiquities of the Jews* 18.5.2.

[4] See Appendix One for a discussion of the translation of this sentence.

reply, Jesus gives a summary of what he is doing. It is as if Jesus is presenting his qualifications to be the one who will be next.

As John's disciples are leaving to convey his answer back to their teacher, Jesus turns to the crowd and praises John: "A prophet? Yes, I tell you, and more than a prophet… Truly, I say to you, among those born of women there has arisen no one greater than John the Baptist." (Matt 11:7, 11).

Soon this man… a man greater than a prophet… greater than Elijah… greater even than Moses… would be beheaded.

But who will be "next"?

Will it be Jesus?

And what does being "next" mean?

The final thing to note about John's question is that, remarkably, it is not about Jesus's current state.

It is about his future.

Part I

The Turning Point

"...the Son of Man must undergo great suffering..."

- Mark 8:31

The cataclysmic change

"I must preach the good news of the kingdom of
God… for I was sent for this purpose."

- Luke 4:43.

After the arrest of John the Baptist, Jesus started on his mission,
and he was crystal clear about what that mission was: preaching the
kingdom of God.[5]

And he didn't just talk the talk – he walked the walk. Literally. He
was out there on the dusty road preaching to crowds. He was privately
instructing his disciples and guiding them on the path of inner
evolution. Many of his followers were women – which in itself
subjected him to all sorts of rumors. He was also training some of his
disciples as emissaries and sending them out in pairs to extend the
range of his mission. If this was all he did, chances are that history
would have accorded him a level of fame less than that of John the
Baptist – i.e., less than almost none.

But John the Baptist is executed by Herod. This has an immediate
and deep effect on Jesus. Suddenly, instead of wanting to preach to
crowds, Jesus tries to avoid them. He takes the disciples away from the
mission of preaching the kingdom of God (Mark 6:31-32). He even
sends the disciples away so that he can be alone and pray alone on a
mountain (Mark 6:46). He then tries to escape the crowds by going
with his disciples to Gennesaret (Mark 6:53). The crowds recognize
him there, so he moves on to Tyre where he again seeks to be
unnoticed and anonymous (Mark 7:24).

These abrupt radical changes are only preludes to far more
dramatic changes. Without any forewarning, Jesus totally abandons his
mission of preaching the kingdom of God. Instead, he sets his face to
Jerusalem and crucifixion and he starts talking about an apocalyptic
reckoning of souls which will come after his death and be led by "the
Son of Man".

So what happened to Jesus? What could possibly have happened
to him that could have caused such wild changes??

------

[5] The meaning of his teachings is explained in *The Jesus Code*.

The Gospels do not record what caused the changes but they do record the changes.

Suddenly Jesus attempts to prepare the disciples for an entirely new vision of who he is and what he has to do. The Gospel of Luke (9:18) records Jesus as praying alone and, when he finishes, he immediately broaches conversation with his disciples.

> "Who do people say that I am?" And they answered him, "John the Baptist; and others, Elijah; and still others, one of the prophets."
>
> - Mark 8:27-28

This is a discussion about whether he could be a great prophet sent back from the dead. Jesus doesn't agree or disagree. Instead he asks another question: "But who do you say that I am?"

Peter answered him, "You are the Messiah."

Again Jesus doesn't agree or disagree. Instead he sternly orders them not to tell anyone his secrets – because he is about to tell them a big one.[6] Jesus tells his disciples of a new mission, a second mission that has nothing to do with preaching the kingdom of God.

---

[6] The standardized paragraphing of the Bible has Peter saying "You are the Messiah" and Jesus immediately follows this with "And he strictly charged them to tell no one about him." (Mark 8:30). End of that paragraph; start of a new one. The original Gospel manuscripts did not have any paragraphing; all the sentences just ran one after the other. The standard paragraphing is a doctrinal paragraphing which makes it sound like Jesus was admonishing Peter to not give away his secret that he was the Messiah. The alternative paragraphing makes much more sense: he was cautioning the disciples not to give away the huge secret he is about to tell them. This is what people standardly do when about to share a secret: "Okay I am about to tell you something important but don't tell anyone." It seems that the disciples adhered to these instructions because there is no mention of non-disciples knowing about this plan.

Moreover, Peter clearly did not take what Jesus said next as an endorsement of his bizarre idea that Jesus was the Messiah. After witnessing the amazing spectacle of Transfiguration, Peter does not call Jesus "Messiah" but rather "Rabbi" (teacher). (Mark 9:5).

> Then he began to teach them that the Son of Man
> must undergo great suffering... and be killed...
>
> - Mark 8:31

This floors the disciples. This presages the loss of their teacher, their mentor, their inspiration, their leader.

> And Peter took him aside and began to rebuke
> him.
>
> - Mark 8:32

(So much for Peter understanding the nature and mission of Jesus.)

Jesus did not need anyone else voicing his own inner doubts.

> But turning and seeing his disciples, he rebuked
> Peter and said, "Get behind me, Satan! For you are
> not setting your mind on the things of God, but
> on the things of man."
>
> - Mark 8:33

Immediately after this interchange – for the first time but certainly not for the last time – Jesus starts talking about a forthcoming apocalyptic reckoning of souls that would be led not by Jesus but by someone else, "the Son of Man":

> "For whoever is ashamed of me and of my words
> in this adulterous and sinful generation, of him will
> the Son of Man also be ashamed when he comes
> in the glory of his Father with the holy angels."
>
> - Mark 8:38.

A handful of days after these stunning revelations, the Gospel of Mark records what is now known as "the Transfiguration".

> And after six days Jesus took with him Peter and
> James and John, and led them up a high mountain
> by themselves. And he was transfigured before

them, and his clothes became radiant, intensely white, as no one on earth could bleach them.

- Mark 9:2-4

Four dramatic events have come in close succession:
1. The execution of John the Baptist (Mark 6:14-29)
2. The announcement by Jesus that he would head to Jerusalem to suffer and die (Mark 8:31)
3. The first mention by Jesus of a forthcoming apocalyptic reckoning of souls to be led by the Son of Man (Mark 8:38)
4. Transfiguration (Mark 9:2-4).

The natural conclusion is that, somehow, these four things are connected.

But how?

The Apocalyptic Son of Man

In the Gospel of Mark, the most historically reliable gospel, Jesus does not say anything at all about a forthcoming apocalyptic reckoning of souls until after the turning point.

"…and you will see the Son of Man seated at the right hand of Power, and coming with the clouds of heaven."

- Mark 14:62

Likewise, in the Gospel of Luke, there is no reference to an apocalyptic Son of Man until after the turning point.

"…but on the day when Lot went out from Sodom, fire and sulfur rained from heaven and destroyed them all – so will it be on the day when the Son of Man is revealed."

- Luke 17:29-30[7]

---

[7] The Gospel of Matthew is notorious for being free and easy in its handling of chronological order.

In *The Jesus Code*, I argued that Jesus used the expression "Son of Man'" to refer to a transformed soul – one that had been transformed by baptism-by-Spirit. But, after the turning point, Jesus begins to often use the expression "the Son of Man" to refer to a specific third person who would lead an apocalyptic reckoning of souls:

> "And then they will see the Son of Man coming in clouds with great power and glory. And then he will send out the angels and gather his elect from the four winds, from the ends of the earth to the ends of heaven."
>
> > \- Mark 13:26-7

> "The harvest is the close of the age, and the reapers are angels. Just as the weeds are gathered and burned with fire, so will it be at the close of the age. The Son of Man will send his angels, and they will gather out of his kingdom all causes of sin and all law-breakers, and throw them into the fiery furnace."
>
> > \- Matthew 13:39-42

But Jesus did not preach this scary apocalyptic message to the masses. This dark vision was virtually exclusively reserved for his inner sanctum of disciples. Across all the Gospels, there is only one time when Jesus may have made a reference to the apocalyptic "Son of Man" in public and it is Jesus's first reference to him:

> "For whoever is ashamed of me and of my words in this adulterous and sinful generation, of him will the Son of Man also be ashamed when he comes in the glory of his Father with the holy angels."
>
> > \- Mark 8:38

The Gospel of Matthew has this spoken to just his disciples (Matt 16:24-28). The Gospel of Luke has it said to "all" which in this context seems to mean all the disciples (Luke 9:23-26). Only the Gospel of Mark indicates that this speech was given to more than the disciples: "calling the crowd to him with his disciples" (Mark 8:34).

If our modern version of the Gospel of Mark is the accurate report here then this is the one and only time that Jesus mentions the apocalyptic Son of Man to the general public. All other references to the apocalyptic "Son of Man" are made in private to his disciples[8] or at his trial to his accusers[9]. If Jesus did blurt this out in public this one time, he obviously thought better of it and thereafter reserved such conversations to private ones with his disciples.

So who or what was Jesus referring to when he referenced this mysterious apocalyptic "Son of Man"?

As always, in understanding Jesus, it is salutary to keep in mind the towering figure of John the Baptist. Jesus trod in the footsteps of his teacher, John the Baptist. Surely baptism by the Holy Spirit happened to John before it happened to Jesus – which is why he was able to refer to it before he ever met Jesus (Mark 1:8).

Jesus's key new expressions "the Holy Spirit" and "the kingdom of God" came directly from John. Surely this third new expression "Son of Man" also came from John and that, as Jesus would after him, John the Baptist had sometimes referred to himself (more particularly, his transformed soul) as "Son of Man".

Jesus rated John the Baptist as equal to or higher than himself. John was the greatest of all born of women (Matthew 11:11). John was the original preacher of the kingdom of God (Luke 16:16). John was the founder, the teacher, the originator. Jesus would be nailed to the cross, believing that John was greater than him.

As far as Jesus knew, John the Baptist was the first ever "Son of Man' – the first ever person to experience baptism-by-Spirit and have his soul fused to spirit – the first ever soul to enter the kingdom of God. He wasn't just "a Son of Man"; he was "the Son of Man".

But now John was dead – freshly executed by Herod.

So we are led towards this conclusion: Jesus's "the Son of Man" who would lead the forthcoming apocalyptic reckoning of souls was the spirit of the recently departed John the Baptist. It was he who would be the right hand of God.

---

[8] Mark 13:26. Matthew 10:23, 13:41, 16:27, 16:28, 19:28, 24:27, 24:30 (twice), 24:37, 24:39, 24:44, 25:31. Luke 9:26, 12:18, 12:40, 17:22, 17:24, 17:26, 17:30, 18:8, 21:27, 21:36. There are no apocalyptic uses of the phrase "Son of Man" in the Gospel of John.

[9] Mark 14:62; Matt 26:64, Luke 22:69.

> "For whoever is ashamed of me and of my words
> in this adulterous and sinful generation, of him will
> the Son of Man also be ashamed when he comes
> in the glory of his Father with the holy angels."

Jesus was absolutely certain his teachings and the apocalyptic Son of Man were in total alignment. There was only one being in heaven and earth in whom Jesus could have had this level of absolute confidence: his teacher, John the Baptist.

In a virtually identical way, in the Gospel of Luke, Jesus affirms the alignment between himself and the Son of Man:

> "And I tell you, everyone who acknowledges me
> before men, the Son of Man also will acknowledge
> before the angels of God, but the one who denies
> me before men will be denied before the angels of
> God." (12:8-9)

For Jesus, it was to be the baptized-by-Spirit soul of John the Baptist – the first ever "Son of Man"– who would be at the right hand of power, leading the way in a forthcoming reckoning of souls. Indeed, it is quite likely that even some of Jesus's earlier, non-apocalyptic uses of the term "Son of Man" – uses which are traditionally taken as self-referential – were actually references to John the Baptist. For instance, when Jesus says:

> "But that you may know that the Son of Man has
> authority on earth to forgive sins"—he said to the
> paralytic— "I say to you, rise, pick up your bed,
> and go home."
>
> - Mark 2:10-11

This incident happens very very shortly after Jesus starts his ministry – when he was still very much preaching under the shadow of the recently-arrested John the Baptist. It is usually taken as Jesus talking about himself as having authority to forgive sins but it is more likely that he was referencing the power of the original "Son of Man", John the Baptist. We know from the Jewish historian Josephus that John the Baptist absolved sins by baptism in water. (See Appendix Two). So here Jesus was likely referencing the power of the original

Son of Man – John the Baptist – to absolve sins.

Likewise, when Jesus says: "So the Son of Man is lord even of the Sabbath" (Mark 2:28), he may well again have been referencing not himself but John the Baptist as lord of the Sabbath. This could indicate that John the Baptist treated the Sabbath like any other day. This is quite likely, as we saw in *The Jesus Code,* that both John and Jesus believed that the Old Covenant was dead and so the Sabbath day was no longer sacrosanct.

So why didn't Jesus at some stage mention to his inner circle of disciples that this apocalyptic Son of Man was the soul of his recently departed teacher, John the Baptist?

The answer is: he probably did… and it got buried.

John the Baptist was the figure who most discomforted writers of the Gospels. Jesus went out to the wilderness to be baptized in water by John and, in his time with him, was baptized by the Holy Spirit. All four Biblical Gospels go to ludicrous lengths to explain this away and make it seem that John the Baptist was inferior to Jesus.[10]

If Jesus did mention to his disciples that the first-ever, right-hand-of-God Son of Man was John the Baptist, this is exactly the information that would have got buried because it would have been rock-solid proof that John the Baptist had spiritual primacy over Jesus. That information would never be allowed to appear in the Gospels which wanted to evidence that Jesus was the one-and-only Messiah and the one-and-only Son of God.

You will recall that there were four events which came in close succession:

1. The execution of John the Baptist;
2. The announcement by Jesus that he would head to Jerusalem to suffer and be killed;
3. The first mention by Jesus of a forthcoming apocalyptic reckoning of souls to be led by "the Son of Man";
4. Transfiguration.

We have now linked two of these: the death of John the Baptist and sudden references to an apocalyptic Son of Man who would lead a reckoning of souls.

---

[10] See "Jesus Delusion I: John the Baptist was a butler announcing Jesus's coming" (below) and see *The Jesus Code*, Part I: John and Jesus.

Let us turn our attention to Transfiguration.

Transfiguration

The Transfiguration of Jesus is one of the most intriguing incidents in the whole story of Jesus. Academic Biblical historians largely roundly ignore it. *Oh, that never really happened.* It is more-or-less lumped in with miracles like walking on water: *Could not have happened.* Yet it records something not miraculous but spiritual.

Moreover, it meets the favored academic "Criterion of Dissimilarity" – it is simply not something that a true believer would invent because, for faith-based Christians, the Transfiguration of Jesus serves no purpose and makes no sense. In the Gospels of Matthew and Luke, Jesus became the Son of God at his birth. In the Gospel of Mark, Jesus became the Son of God when he experienced Baptism by the Holy Spirit. So why would a true believer make up this bizarre incident of Transfiguration? Why would the Son of God need any further spiritual transformation??

The Gospel most concerned to paint Jesus as the Son of God for all eternity – the Gospel of John – leaves this awkward incident out.

The three Synoptic Gospels make no suggestion as to what was the purpose of Transfiguration. Indeed, in the two thousand years since, no Christian theologian has ever made a really plausible suggestion as to why it was needed.

What purpose could it have served???

Remember John the Baptist's enigmatic question sent out to Jesus: "Are you the one who is to be next or shall we look for another?"

Could it have been that it was Transfiguration which John was referring to?

For John to go to the enormous trouble of sending disciples out to track down Jesus in order to ask him this one solitary question, it would have to be a question about something truly momentous. Obviously the question wasn't about crucifixion. Apart from that, the only other momentous thing which will happen to Jesus after that time is Transfiguration.

Was John asking whether Jesus had been tapped on his spiritual shoulder and received some message indicating that Jesus was the one to be "next"? The next one to be Transfigured after the death of John?

This has profound implications.

First, it indicates that Jesus was not the only candidate for Transfiguration – that there were others out there who were possible candidates. Presumably these were other students of John the Baptist who had undergone Baptism by the Holy Spirit and so were possible candidates for Transfiguration. If Jesus was not The One, they would go on to ask others.

Second, it indicates that only one person at a time can be Transfigured.

Third, it indicates that John the Baptist had been Transfigured and that, after his death, someone else – one other person only – would be "next".

Again, we have to contemplate that the student did not exceed the master. Just as John was baptized by the Holy Spirit before Jesus ever set his face to the wilderness, likewise John was Transfigured before Jesus ever came on the scene. But, unlike Baptism by the Holy Spirit, it seems that, at any one time, only one person can be Transfigured. John, facing the inevitability of death, wanted to know who would be next after him. "Are you the one who is to be next or shall we look for another?"

Let us look at some of the recorded details of the Transfiguration of Jesus.

> …Jesus took with him Peter and James and John, and led them up a high mountain by themselves. And he was transfigured before them, and his clothes became radiant, intensely white, as no one on earth could bleach them. And there appeared to them Elijah with Moses, and they were talking with Jesus.
>
> - Mark 9:2-4

There is simply no way that these three disciples could have recognized the two figures as having been Moses and Elijah. It is not like the disciples ever saw photos of those two legendary figures. What they saw were two figures who looked like prophets of old. So consider this possibility: could one of these astral figures been that of the recently departed John the Baptist?

We know that John looked like a prophet of old: wild beard and wild hair. Moreover, both John the Baptist and Elijah are described as wearing hair with a leather belt (2 Kings 1:8; Mark 1:6). As such, any figure that looked like Elijah would also have been the image of John the Baptist.

(Note that these three disciples had been fishermen from the shores of the Sea of Galilee who were called by Jesus after the arrest of John the Baptist. It is unlikely that they ever saw the Baptist.[11])

What is the first thing that Jesus mentions after his Transfiguration?

The Son of Man (i.e., John the Baptist) and his return.

> And as they were coming down the mountain, he charged them to tell no one what they had seen, until the Son of Man had risen from the dead. So they kept the matter to themselves, questioning what this rising from the dead might mean.
>
> - Mark 9:9-10

This adds enormous weight to the theory that one of the figures seen with Jesus looked like a legendary prophet of old but was actually the spirit of John the Baptist, the Son of Man, who was to come back from the dead.

Remarkably, Jesus then immediately goes on to draw a direct comparison between Elijah and John the Baptist (the Son of Man), both of whom had suffered and been treated with contempt:

> And they asked him, "Why do the scribes say that first Elijah must come?" And he said to them, "Elijah does come first to restore all things. And how is it written of the Son of Man that he should suffer many things and be treated with contempt? But I tell you that Elijah has come, and they did to him whatever they pleased, as it is written of him."
>
> - Mark 9:11-13

This could indicate that Jesus believed that the two figures that were with him during Transfiguration were Elijah and John the Baptist.

---

[11] See Mark 1:16-20. The "Simon" referred to in this passage later had his name changed to Peter.

Again, if Jesus ever did specifically clarify to his disciples that the spirit of John the Baptist was present at the Transfiguration, this would have been suppressed.

So we now have links between the death of John the Baptist, the apocalyptic Son of Man and the Transfiguration of Jesus.

But what is Transfiguration?

Why can it only happen to one person at a time?

And how is it linked to Jesus's decision to go to Jerusalem, suffer and die?

God in the kingdom of God

Baptism by the Holy Spirit is referenced by different mystics in different ways: Union with the One, Divine Marriage, Union with the Lord of Love, etc. John the Baptist and Jesus often referred to it in terms of "the kingdom of God": when a soul is fused with the Holy Spirit, it enters into the kingdom of God – it is no longer cut off from God, no longer inaccessible to him.[12] This then gives an indication of what Transfiguration could be: the connection of God with a transformed soul. When a soul experiences Baptism by the Holy Spirit, it becomes a "Son of Man" and enters into the Kingdom of God/heaven. This makes possible the connection of God the Father with a Son of Man such as John the Baptist or Jesus:

> The Father was in the Son and the Son in the
> Father. This is the Kingdom of Heaven.
>
> - Gospel of Philip 102, WI

Transfiguration can only be made sense of as being the connection of God with the transformed soul of Jesus. Otherwise, it serves no purpose and makes no sense. As much as possible, at the Transfiguration, God drew into the soul of Jesus. No wonder that "…the appearance of his face was altered, and his clothing became dazzling white." (Luke 9:29)

Such a connection, such a divine focus, can only happen with one soul at a time.

---

[12] See *The Jesus Code*.

This also provides an explanation of why the soul of John the Baptist was present at the Transfiguration. It was the transfer of the connection with God from John's soul to Jesus's soul.

But why would God do this? Why would God want to make such a close connection to a soul? To one soul and only one soul at a time? What would God get out of doing this?

And why did God want Jesus to suffer and die? Not just die. Suffer terrible agony and die.

Later, in Gethsemane, Jesus would prostrate himself and repeatedly beg God to release him from the suffering. As a mystic, he was not frightened of death but, like any sane person, he did not want to go through hours – perhaps even days – of unimaginable physical torment.

But God did not let him off the hook.

Why did God need Jesus to suffer? If the game was the "rise again after three days", that does not require suffering. Quick, painless death and then back again three days later. So why the extreme suffering of the Cross?

To understand why God needed Jesus to suffer, we need to understand the nature of suffering, and we need to better understand the nature of God.

The Lot of Man: Suffering

God is all-powerful and inviolate. He can do anything, right?

Actually, there is one thing which Man can do which God cannot. Suffer.

More particularly: experience unjustified suffering. Pretty much all animals are capable of physical suffering. Some animals are also capable of emotional suffering. But perhaps only Man is capable of feeling his suffering as unjustified.

Sometimes a person is born with a rare genetic condition known as "congenital analgesia" so that they can feel no physical pain at all. It is a dangerous condition because you could cut yourself, get an infection and die – and never even have noticed that you were cut.

Imagine you were not only born with this condition but, in addition, you were also born an extreme psychopath so that you could also feel no emotional pain.

You would then never experience either physical or emotional pain: no fear, no depression, no frustration, no heartbreak, no anger at injustice. But then you would also not be able to feel the positive things that those negative things lead to: patience, tolerance, composure, courage, compassion.

How could you possibly understand what the rest of humanity was going through?

You couldn't.

You would not have the foggiest idea about the experiences of the rest of humanity.

Imagine you are God.

You are all-powerful. You are inviolate and invulnerable. You cannot feel physical or emotional pain. You cannot feel frustration. You cannot feel heartbreak or fear or depression or anger at injustice. And you cannot feel the positive things that those negative things lead to: patience, tolerance, composure, courage, compassion. You cannot understand what it is to be human.

Until you experience suffering, you cannot understand the lot of man.

In the astonishing *Book of Job*, this is what Job accuses God of: a comprehensive inability to understand Man. "Does it seem good to you to oppress, to despise the work of your hands and favor the designs of the wicked? Have you eyes of flesh? Do you see as man sees?" (Job 10:3-4; KJV)

This is what God could not do. He could not see with eyes of flesh. He could not suffer as man suffers. He could not understand the lot of Man.

How could the infinite, the invulnerable, the all-powerful understand the finite, the vulnerable, the powerless, the suffering?

Ah, but now there was a way... the Holy Spirit. The Spirit that runs through all things – through all souls and God. That great spiritual field could connect God to an incarnated soul in man. But only... ONLY... if that soul had been baptized-by-Spirit. Only then would a soul become part of the kingdom of God, a place which God could connect to.

Via such a transformed soul dwelling in the body of a Man – via a "Son of Man" – God could experience as a man experiences. Then God could experience the one thing absolutely necessary for him to understand Man: unjustified suffering.

34

God needed a Son of Man to suffer. Really suffer. To endure terrible unjustified torment. Jesus was to be a conduit for God to understand the Lot of Man.

> Since God's Son could not suffer in the divinity and in eternity, the heavenly Father sent him into time so that he should become human and could suffer.
>
> - Meister Eckhart, *Selected Writings*, p.84.

If you are a typical faith-based Christian (or Muslim or anyone who believes in an all-powerful God), your head may now be reeling. *God is God. He can do anything. He understands everything.*

But if you can DO everything, can you EXPERIENCE everything?

You can't.

If you are all-powerful, how can you experience the sensation and frustration of powerlessness? If you are invulnerable, how can you experience fear and weakness?

You can't… at least, not by yourself. You can only experience it via someone else – via someone who can experience vulnerability, fear and weakness. God could experience all these things but only via a transformed, baptized-by-Spirit soul (a Son of Man).

God's education had started with John the Baptist. God experienced the sufferings of John: the privations in the wilderness, the arrest, the horrors of incarceration, the beheading. This perhaps explains why John was so abstemious – living off locusts and wild honey, wearing camel hair, enduring the harshness of the wilderness – because he wanted God to experience the privations that human flesh is heir to. This also clarifies why Jesus said: "From Adam to John the Baptist, among those born of women, no one is so much greater than John the Baptist that his eyes should not be averted." (Gospel of Thomas 46) Truly their eyes should be averted because, though they didn't know it, they were in the presence of the vessel that was carrying the connection to God.

Moreover, this also explains why God needed such a horrific level of suffering from Jesus. He had already experienced a level of suffering through John. God needed to take his understanding of human suffering to the next level, the ultimate level of physical suffering and death: the agony of crucifixion.

Transfiguration was the launching point of this new mission for Jesus – a mission bigger by far than his first mission of preaching the kingdom of God.

His new mission was to educate God.

The kingdom of God is within you

This yields up the definitive explanation of why John the Baptist coined his unique expression "the kingdom of God".

Other mystics do not favor this sort of expression; but John knew from first-hand experience that baptism by the Holy Spirit made his soul part of the domain of God: transforming it into something that God could connect to, enter into and, via which, God could experience the lot of Man. John the Baptist saw this as a totally new phenomenon. God had drawn close to man, seeking to connect to him. For the first time in all eternity, the kingdom of God was nigh:

> "The time is fulfilled, and the kingdom of God is
> at hand… believe in the good news."
>
> - Mark 1:15

There is a fascinating passage in Luke which indicates that Jesus fully understood that John had pioneered the way for God to enter into a temple within human souls. It happens just after the enquiry about whether Jesus was the one who was to be next:

> When John's messengers had gone, Jesus began to speak to the crowds concerning John: "What did you go out into the wilderness to see? A reed shaken by the wind? What then did you go out to see? A man dressed in soft clothing? Behold, those who are dressed in splendid clothing and live in luxury are in kings' courts. What then did you go out to see? A prophet? Yes, I tell you, and more than a prophet."
>
> - Luke 7:24-26.

"Prophet" (in Hebrew "*navi*") means "spokesperson" – i.e., a spokesperson for God. Jesus was saying that John was more than a mouthpiece for God. How can anyone be greater than being a spokesperson for God? But, if you have been Transfigured and are carrying the connection with God, then you are much more than a mouthpiece. No wonder Jesus says: "I tell you, among those born of women none is greater than John" (Luke 7:28).

Jesus goes on to say of John:

> "This is he of whom it is written,
> 'Behold, I send my messenger before your face,
> who will prepare your way before you.'"
>
> - Luke 7:27.

This looks to be a deliberate misquoting of Jesus to make it look like John the Baptist was just preparing the way for Jesus. The actual passage is from Malachi (3:1) and it is the Lord God speaking and it reads like this:

> "Behold, I send my messenger, and he will prepare
> the way before me. And the Lord whom you seek
> will suddenly come to his temple..."

If, as is far more likely, Jesus originally quoted the Malachi passage correctly, Jesus was saying that John the Baptist had prepared and pioneered the way *for God* to come into his temple – that temple being a transformed soul that had now become part of the kingdom of God.

Consider this description of John the Baptist at the start of the Gospel of Mark (1:3):

> the voice of one crying in the wilderness:
> "Prepare the way of the Lord,
> make his paths straight"

This is invariably interpreted as John the Baptist having been sent solely for the purpose of preparing things for the Lord Jesus. This interpretation is extraordinarily fanciful because not one disciple in the entire Gospel of Mark addresses the living Jesus as "Lord".[13] Indeed, when he enters Jerusalem, they refer to Jesus not as "Lord" but as "he who comes in the name of the Lord" (Mark 11:9). The original passage from Isaiah (40:3) is actually about someone preparing the way for the Lord God:

> A voice cries:
> "In the wilderness prepare the way of the Lord;
> make straight in the desert a highway for our God."

And this is what John the Baptist did do for God: he pioneered a pathway for God to connect to incarnate baptized-by-spirit souls. And John the Baptist cried out for others to come out to the wilderness and do likewise: prepare a highway in their souls for the Lord. It may be that it was consideration of this very passage in Isaiah which convinced John that the right place for his ministry was in the wilderness.

The Birth of the New Covenant

Transfiguration is what stands out as truly unique about John the Baptist and Jesus. Not baptism by the Holy Spirit, for we have seen that other mystics have written about the fusion of soul with spirit. But Transfiguration – God "entering into" or connecting to a transformed soul – that is not referenced by other mystics.

We have also seen that, seemingly unique among mystics, John the Baptist and Jesus believed that what was happening to them indicated that an apocalyptic reckoning of souls was on the way. So we are inexorably led to consider that these two things were linked: Transfiguration and their belief in an imminent reckoning of souls.

Why would Transfiguration bring about a conviction that a reckoning of souls was coming?

Transfiguration marks the connection of God to a transformed soul created through baptism by the Holy Spirit. God was going to have human experiences via John the Baptist and then Jesus. In

---

[13] This does not include any passages after Mark 16:8 which scholars agree is the original endpoint of the Gospel of Mark.

particular, he was going to experience that most quintessential of human experiences: unjustified suffering. In so doing, God would come to understand humanity. He would understand the true horrors of man's inhumanity to man. He would become capable of empathy and compassion. So he should then act.

He must act.

He would act.

Surely.

God would cease to be the blood-and-thunder heartless God of the Old Testament and become instead a God of compassion.

Consider the horrors of the Jewish Holocaust in the 20th Century - one of the most shameful, disgraceful events in the entire benighted history of humanity. Millions of Jews rounded up by the Nazis, starved, worked to death, beaten, tortured, gassed. Children, still living, thrown into the ovens of Auschwitz.

During this time, some Jews lost their faith in God. What had become of the Mosaic covenant with God? How could any God allow such horrors to happen?

How indeed?

Consider the horrors that go on today. Babies and children are raped. Innocent people tortured. How could a compassionate God who truly understood human suffering let such horrors and injustice go on?

How indeed?

Surely a compassionate God who understood human suffering would intervene to wipe out the worst of souls.

Isn't that what you would do if you had the power? Wouldn't you stop children being raped? Wouldn't you put an end to innocent people being tortured? Wouldn't you? If you had the power to stop it, could you really sit back and just watch children being raped? Could you??

Could you???

I couldn't.

Surely a God who now understood human suffering would intervene to wipe out the worst of evils on the planet.

This then is the new covenant which John the Baptist and Jesus came to believe in: that, via them, God would experience human suffering and, as a result, God would come to understand the Lot of Man/Woman and become capable of compassion. A now-compassionate God would intervene with a reckoning of souls. He would act and would wipe out the evil-doers on the planet. This would be the gift that humankind would receive under the new covenant: souls that had been baptized-by-Spirit would be spared and so also would souls with some level of compassion towards others because they had some chance of bearing fruit and being baptized by Spirit. But the remainder of souls – the ones with no promise of bearing fruit – the irredeemable souls – would be culled. Annihilated.

John the Baptist had been the start of God's experiential learning curve. Jesus was the next conduit for God's understanding of suffering. Jesus would throw himself upon the cross so that God would understand the ultimate in human physical suffering: crucifixion. His sacrifice was to be "a ransom for many".

> "For even the Son of Man came not to be served but to serve, and to give his life as a ransom for many."
>
> - Mark 10:45

This statement could be held to be equally true of two Sons of Man: Jesus and John the Baptist.

What is a ransom?

It is a price paid in order to liberate innocents from captivity by evil ones.

This is how Jesus saw the human impact of his sacrifice on the Cross: not as something that would benefit everyone but as something that would benefit the many who were in the clutches of evil. His suffering and death were never going to wipe out the sins of all; instead it would liberate many. The hopeless, cruel, evil and irredeemably selfish souls would be wiped out by a now compassionate God who understood suffering. Jesus's suffering and death would then be a "ransom" paid to liberate the many who suffer under the jackboot of evil-doers.

This was the New Covenant.

The Old Covenant of Moses has been sealed by blood. After Moses brought down the Ten Commandments from the mountain, he read them out to the Israelites and then read out the rest of the Law. He then sealed the covenant between man and God in blood:

Moses came and told the people all the words of the Lord and all the rules. And all the people answered with one voice and said, "All the words that the Lord has spoken we will do." And Moses wrote down all the words of the Lord. He rose early in the morning and built an altar at the foot of the mountain, and twelve pillars, according to the twelve tribes of Israel. And he sent young men of the people of Israel, who offered burnt offerings and sacrificed peace offerings of oxen to the Lord. And Moses took half of the blood and put it in basins, and half of the blood he threw against the altar. Then he took the Book of the Covenant and read it in the hearing of the people. And they said, "All that the Lord has spoken we will do, and we will be obedient." And Moses took the blood and threw it on the people and said, "Behold the blood of the covenant that the Lord has made with you in accordance with all these words."

- Exodus 24:3-8

Jesus, knowing that he was going to suffer and bleed and die on the Cross, saw his blood as sealing the New Covenant. He says as much at the Last Supper:

And he said to them, "This is my blood of the covenant, which is poured out for many."

- Mark 14:24.

The New Covenant was to be sealed by the blood of Jesus. On a cross.

So what happened at the turning point?

So what could have happened to Jesus at the turning point that was so dramatic that it convinced him to abandon his mission of preaching the kingdom of God?

Something so intense that it convinced him that an apocalyptic reckoning of souls was on the way and it would be led by the Son of Man?

Something so cataclysmic that it convinced Jesus to climb a mountain and accept Transfiguration?

Something so real that it convinced Jesus to seek out and submit to the agony of crucifixion???

Flash forward: The resurrection of Jesus

Only a handful of weeks after the turning point, some people were to be confronted with a shocking, life-changing experience. They would see Jesus after his death.

I will be arguing that those were sightings of the astral body of Jesus – his ghost, his spirit. Astral bodies take on the imprint of the physical body they are/were in.

Jesus's astral body would have been spectacularly vibrant because it had been energized by baptism by the Holy Spirit and by Transfiguration. It was so vibrant that it could even be seen in the daytime. It was so vivid that it convinced many who saw it that Jesus had come back from the dead. It was so real that it convinced some that there would be a Second Coming of Jesus and he would judge souls and resurrect the good ones. Jesus was just the first fruit of the resurrection of the dead.

What likely happened at the turning point

Jesus knew that his teacher, John the Baptist, had been Transfigured and carried the connection with God. That is why he rated John as greater than any prophet... as great as any man who has ever lived.

When Jesus heard John's question *Are you the one who is to be next or shall we look for another?*, Jesus knew what John was asking: he was asking whether Jesus would be the one to take on the connection with God after John's death. But Jesus had not yet received any spiritual message that he would be next. Instead, Jesus puts forward his qualifications to be next after John: "Go and tell John what you hear and see: the blind receive their sight and the lame walk, lepers are cleansed and the deaf hear, and the dead are raised up, and the poor have good news preached to them. And blessed is the one who is not offended by me." (Matt 11:4-6)

So what happened to Jesus that convinced him that he would indeed be next? That he needed to go up a mountain and open himself up to Transfiguration?

Here is my explanation: Jesus was visited by the spirit of his recently departed teacher, John the Baptist.

Just as Jesus's soul would be so John the Baptist's soul was: it was vibrant and luminous. It had been made extraordinarily vibrant by Baptism-by-Spirit and Transfiguration. After the death of his physical body, the Transfigured spirit of John the Baptist visits Jesus. This visitation lets Jesus know that, if he is willing, he is the one who will be next – the next to take on the connection with God and so take on responsibility for the evolution of God. In Jesus's case, he will have to suffer crucifixion so that God can take his understanding of suffering to the next level, the ultimate level.

This visitation convinces Jesus that if he does these things then the soul of John the Baptist, the Son of Man, will lead a reckoning of souls. The most fallen of souls, the most evil of souls, the most hopeless of souls would be wiped out to the benefit of the rest of humanity. Jesus's blood sacrifice would be a ransom for many.

The Gospel of Mark tells us that, very shortly after the death of the Baptist, Jesus went to extraordinary trouble to get away from the crowds and even sent his disciples away so that he could be alone:

> Immediately he made his disciples get into the boat and go before him to the other side, to Bethsaida, while he dismissed the crowd. And after he had taken leave of them, he went up on the mountain to pray.
>
> - Mark 6:45-46.

This is the only time in the Gospel where Jesus shows such an absolute determination to be completely and utterly alone. There must have been a very big reason for it. Now that John was dead, was Jesus trying to commune with the spirit of his departed teacher? Was he trying to be alone so he could find out if he was the one chosen to be next?

We know that the Gospel writers associated mountains with crucial spiritual events: the Beatitudes are announced on a mountain, Transfiguration occurs on a mountain, the Twelve are sent out to preach to greater Israel from a mountain. Mountains are huge in Jewish thought because the Ten Commandments were brought down from a mountain. No Gospel would mention that Jesus went up a mountain to pray alone unless something of a momentous spiritual nature happened on that mountain.

But whatever happened there has been edited out.

There is no mention of what happened on that mountain. It is a huge drum-roll signifying something momentous and dramatic… and… then… nothing…

We know that the incidents which Gospel writers were most likely to leave out or alter were anything which gave John the Baptist the glow of spiritual power.

Could this be when it happened? Could this be when Jesus received a visitation from the spirit of his beloved teacher? [14] Does the

---

[14] Fascinatingly, the Gospel of Mark 6:45-50 records that, on this very night, disciples in a boat see what they believe is a ghost which terrifies them and they do not recognize it. Interesting speculation to consider that what they saw was the spirit (ghost) of John the Baptist and this

spirit of John convey what is involved in being next? That the one who is to be next has to be crucified? Does Jesus then do what any sane person would do? Does he agonize about submitting voluntarily to the torturous death of crucifixion?

Immediately after his time alone on the mountain, Jesus goes to extreme lengths to wiggle out of this fate. He gets his disciples to take him in a boat across to Gennesaret but he is immediately recognized so he rapidly moves on....

> And from there he arose and went away to the region of Tyre and Sidon. And he entered a house and did not want anyone to know, yet he could not be hidden.
>
> - Mark 7:24

That is extraordinary behavior for a public preacher supposedly on a mission of spreading the word about the kingdom of God. Instead, he is trying to be anonymous and invisible. It seems that Jesus was understandably struggling with the decision of accepting Transfiguration and the crucifixion which came with that responsibility.

But, eventually, Jesus does submit. Suddenly he abandons his mission to preach the kingdom of God. He tells the disciples that he must go to Jerusalem, be crucified and die. He begins to talk privately to his disciples about a forthcoming reckoning of souls led by the Son of Man, John the Baptist. He climbs a mountain to accept Transfiguration. There the connection with God is transferred from the soul of John the Baptist to Jesus. Now it is Jesus who has the responsibility for the evolution of God – a responsibility which is to only last a few short weeks but will culminate in the single biggest turning point in the history of humanity.

And so it is that Jesus sets his face towards Jerusalem and crucifixion.

---

later got edited into seeing Jesus. This is the only time there is a reference to anything even vaguely like this prior to Jesus's crucifixion.

Jesus Delusion I

John the Baptist was a butler announcing Jesus's coming

This book and *The Jesus Code* bear witness to the resurrection of the real historical Jesus and his actual teachings and life. They also bear witness to the resurrection of the historical John the Baptist.

There is no doubt that, of all the figures in the New Testament, the one who most discomforted the Gospel writers was John the Baptist. How could the super-divine Jesus have gone out into the wilderness to be baptized by someone else???

Surely a baptizer is spiritually in advance of the one baptized??

That simply could not be.

All four Gospels battled with this discomfort and all four came up with ludicrous answers.

The Gospel of Mark has John declare that he is unworthy to untie Jesus's sandals and that, unlike himself, Jesus would baptize people with the Holy Spirit (Mark 1:7-8). But, across all four Gospels, there is no record of the living Jesus ever baptizing anyone with the Holy Spirit. By contrast, Jesus was baptized by the Holy Spirit under the supervision of John (Mark 1:9-11).

The Gospel of Matthew has John tell Jesus that he should baptize him rather than vice-versa (Matt 3:13-15).

The Gospel of Luke turns John into a cousin of Jesus and has him filled with the Holy Spirit before he was born (Luke 1:13-15). Even as an unborn baby, John recognizes the divinity of the pregnant Mary (Luke 1:39-45).

The Gospel of John dodges around actually describing a baptism of Jesus by John the Baptist. Instead, it records John the Baptist as bearing witness to Jesus having being baptized by the Holy Spirit (John 1:29-34).

Yet this is the man whom Jesus rated:

- the highest of all born of women (Matt 11:11)
- greater than the prophets of old (Luke 7:26)
- the originator of the teaching of the kingdom of God (Luke 16:16).

John the Baptist is the first person to ever mention "the kingdom of God", "Holy Spirit" and baptism by the Holy Spirit (Mark 1:8; Matt 3:2,11; Luke 3:16). Almost certainly Jesus's other key expression "Son of Man" also came from his teacher, John the Baptist. It was John who taught the "Lord's Prayer" to Jesus who in turn passed it on to his own disciples (Luke 11:1-4). Likewise Jesus's teachings of the Beatitudes and many of his parables almost certainly came straight from John.

John the Baptist was so revered that the chief priests in Jerusalem dared not speak against him lest common folk heard about it (Mark 11:27-33).

His influence was so widespread that, decades after the death of Jesus, Paul came across a community of followers of John the Baptist in the city of Ephesus in what is now Turkey (Acts 19:1-3). Even down to the present day, the highly secretive Mandaean people/sect have John the Baptist as their primary prophet and regard Jesus as a deviance from the real teaching.[15]

John the Baptist was so revered that when Herod's army suffered a devastating defeat, the people said it was God's punishment for Herod having imprisoned and executed John (Josephus, *Antiquities of the Jews* 18.5.2).

His spiritual power was so feared that Herod was frightened that he would come back from the dead (Mark 6:14-16).

This was no milksop butler hanging around to announce the forthcoming entry of someone else. This was the towering pioneer of the mystic path for the Israelite people.

On the basis that the student did not exceed the master, we would have to conclude that:

- John the Baptist himself had experienced Baptism by the Holy Spirit. How else could he have known about it prior to even meeting Jesus? (Mark 1:8)
- John the Baptist experienced Transfiguration which is why he described a baptized soul as becoming part of "the kingdom of God".
- If Jesus's soul could be vibrantly seen after his death (to be discussed in Part V), then so too could the soul of John the Baptist after his death.

---

[15] See the Wikipedia articles on Mandaeans and Mandaeaism.

- If that is the case then what turned Jesus away from preaching the kingdom of God and towards crucifixion could have been a visitation by the spirit of his recently departed teacher.
- It is immediately after this turning point that Jesus starts talking for the first time about an apocalyptic Son of Man whose beliefs are in direct alignment with his own teachings (Mark 8:38). Surely this could only refer to the soul of his recently departed teacher.
- An Elijah-like figure seen at the Transfiguration of Jesus was likely the soul of John the Baptist which is why Jesus afterwards immediately refers to "the Son of Man" (Mark 9:2-13).

This then is the towering figure of John the Baptist: the teacher of Jesus, revered by the people, feared by the priesthood, and dreaded by Herod.

Of course, we are still left with many puzzles about John. What techniques for inner spiritual evolution did he use?

We don't know.

Where did John get his start on his inner journey? Did he perhaps start off as an Essene? Perhaps in the Dead Sea community at Qumran?[16] A case could be made for this:

- The Essenes were a very dedicated Jewish sect with a strong emphasis on purification in water. John baptized in water and, according to the Jewish historian Josephus, John's ministry was all about purification.17
- Both the Essenes and John believed in an end-of-days scenario.18

---

[16] For an introduction to the Essenes and the Dead Sea Scrolls, see the relevant articles in Wikipedia. There is a possibility that the Dead Sea Quran community were not an "Essene" group but a similar yet different group. John may have come from the Qumran community or an Essene group situated elsewhere in the "wilderness".

[17] See discussion of Josephus in Appendix Two.

[18] See the Dead Sea Scrolls 4Q521 COL. 2:1–13.

- The Essenes believed that their rightful place was in the wilderness, which is also where John conducted his ministry.[19]
- The Dead Sea Scrolls mention "holy spirit" in a number of places[20] which could indicate that John the Baptist derived this term from the Essenes – though John's and Jesus's use of this term is very different.
- Jesus preached the nine Beatitudes to his disciples as their very first lesson: there are eight short Beatitudes and then one longer one. Almost certainly, Jesus is passing on what he has learnt from John the Baptist. The Dead Sea Scrolls (4Q525) contain a list of Beatitudes ("Blessed are…") with a parallel structure. Parts are missing but it seems that there were eight shorter ones followed by a ninth longer one. The content is completely different but the structure is the same. One explanation for this similarity is that John the Baptist internalized this form in his time with the Essenes and then reproduced the structure of it in his formulation of the Beatitudes. This was passed on to Jesus and then recorded as being spoken by him in the Gospel of Matthew.[21]
- The Essenes believed that a new or revised Covenant was coming for the Israelite nation - a covenant that would not be about external practice but about one's inner relationship with God. They based this around Jeremiah 31:31-34. This passage could well be held up as emblematic of the practice and teachings of John the Baptist then Jesus:

---

[19] See the Dead Sea Scrolls: "Rule of the Community" 1QS COL. 8:12–16.

[20] The most interesting passage is one which links the Holy Spirit and purification: "…purifying me by Thy Holy Spirit, and drawing me near to Thee by Thy grace according to the abundance of Thy mercies'. (Hymn 5:VIII in Vermes, *The Complete Dead Sea Scrolls in English*, p. 258.)

[21] See the excellent article by Peter Flint, "Jesus and the Dead Sea Scrolls" in Amy-Jill Levine et al, *The Historical Jesus in Context*, pp. 110-131. You can find a readily accessible comparison of the New Testament Beatitudes with the Dead Sea Scrolls Beatitudes here: bible.ca/manuscripts/bible-manuscripts-dss-dead-sea-scrolls-4Q525-Beatitudes-Jesus-Matthew5-blessed-recognizable-format-structure-8short-1long-50bc.htm

"Behold, the days are coming, declares the Lord, when I will make a new covenant with the house of Israel and the house of Judah, not like the covenant that I made with their fathers on the day when I took them by the hand to bring them out of the land of Egypt, my covenant that they broke, though I was their husband, declares the Lord. For this is the covenant that I will make with the house of Israel after those days, declares the Lord: I will put my law within them, and I will write it on their hearts. And I will be their God, and they shall be my people. And no longer shall each one teach his neighbor and each his brother, saying, 'Know the Lord,' for they shall all know me, from the least of them to the greatest, declares the Lord. For I will forgive their iniquity, and I will remember their sin no more."

- Jeremiah 31:31-34[22]

So there is a very solid case that John started off as an Essene, had the breakthrough experience of baptism by the Holy Spirit, and this caused him to leave that sect to start his own ministry in the wilderness. Or, indeed, he could have been kicked out of their community. The Essenes were very strict – refusing to even defecate on the Sabbath!

Perhaps John the Baptist started off as an Essene but he certainly went beyond what they taught – becoming a revered and even feared spiritual figure. In no way was this man beneath his student who obviously revered him.

Yet… rapidly approaching… was coming a time when this student was going to surpass the master. For Jesus was going to far exceed his teacher in suffering.

---

[22] The Dead Sea Scrolls explicitly reference Jeremiah in the Cairo Damascus Document (CD 8:20-21).

<u>Jesus Delusion II</u>

The weight of the sins of the world

The official Christian line as to why Jesus ended up nailed to a cross is that he was taking on the sins of the world.

This is the primary delusion on which all faith-based Christianity is built: Jesus suffered on the Cross in order to expiate the sins of all souls. This is a catastrophic misapprehension of Jesus's mission. Moreover, the idea is so obviously delusory.

If you're a faith-based Christian, you classically believe these four things:

1. God is all-powerful
2. God is good
3. Jesus was God's son
4. Jesus died in absolute agony on the Cross

But… as God is all-powerful, he can do as he pleases. Anything at all.

Anything.

If God wanted to forgive humanity for its purported "sins", he didn't need to torture his own son to do it. He could have just forgiven humanity. No crown of thorns, no scourging, no nails through soft flesh, no pain, no death. Just forgiveness. That would have been the good and right thing to do.

Jesus himself begged to be spared. "Father, let this cup pass from me."

God spared Abraham's son from sacrifice at the last minute (Genesis 22:1-12); he could have spared Mary's son as well.

What is particularly irritating about the Church espousing this delusion about the "sins of the world" is that, in the main, the leaders of the Catholic Church never actually adhered to its implications. If Jesus expunged all our sins then why the hell did we need confessions and indulgences and making penance? Why were we all still sinners who still needed the Church to rescue us – and keep those donations rolling in...

Part II

The Passion of the Christ

"Remove this cup from me. Yet not what I will, but what you will."

- Mark 14:36

Organizing his own downfall

There is an old Sufi saying: *Trust in God and tether your camels because God has no other hands than yours.*

A lot of faith-based Christians seem to be under the impression that Jesus was psychic, the future was revealed unto him, and it was all pre-ordained. To fulfill his destiny on the Cross at Golgotha, all Jesus had to do was turn up in Jerusalem as it had all been pre-arranged by God.

But that is not the story that the Gospel of Mark tells. Instead it tells the story of a Jesus actively provoking the authorities to crucify him. Embracing his second mission, Jesus sets out to organize what has become known as "the Passion of the Christ". "Passion" is from a Greek word *passio* meaning "to suffer".

It was up to Jesus to organize his suffering because God had no other hands than his.

Getting beheaded like John the Baptist – quick and clean – was not going to do it. It was up to Jesus to take suffering to a new level – the ultimate level. Jesus had to suffer utterly. That meant crucifixion. It seems from the very first moment of his being tapped on the shoulder, Jesus knew that it had to be crucifixion. Immediately after rebuking Peter, Jesus references the cross for the first time:

> And calling the crowd to him with his disciples, he said to them, "If anyone would come after me, let him deny himself and take up his cross and follow me."

> - Mark 8:34

Crucifixion had to be done by Roman hands for only they could crucify someone. And that meant he needed to head to Jerusalem.

> "But I must go on my way today and tomorrow and the next day, because it is impossible that a prophet should be killed outside Jerusalem."

> - Luke 13:33 (ISV)

Jesus chooses to arrive at Jerusalem at the only time of the year that Roman troops were guaranteed to be there: the Passover. The rest of the year, the Romans let the Jewish authorities manage things: *Just send us the taxes, we'll guard the borders, and you call us if you need us.* Other than that, they let the Israelites govern their own affairs. But at the Passover, the Roman Governor of Judea would go in with troops ready to quell any possible disturbance because that was the time of year when disturbances were most likely. The population of Jerusalem would massively swell with Israelites making a special pilgrimage to the Temple.

Moreover, the Passover was an emotional time for the Jews. It marked their liberation from slavery in Egypt. It reminded them that they were back under the yoke of another foreign power – not Egypt now but Rome. The Passover was a time of silent protests – and noisy ones.

That particular Passover, the current Governor, Pontius Pilate, would come to Jerusalem and station troops around the place where a disturbance was most likely: the Temple.

So Jesus turns his face towards Jerusalem at Passover time so he can be crucified by the Romans and suffer unto death.

Having resolved to be crucified, did Jesus do the sensible thing and physically set himself for crucifixion? If you knew you were going to be crucified and had time to prepare for it, wouldn't you physically weaken yourself so that your torment would be over so much faster? Perhaps starving yourself of food so that you would be nailed to the cross in a badly weakened state? Possibly this is what Jesus did do which may explain why his crucifixion was mercifully brief: hours rather than days.

The Imitation of Christ

"Messiah" originally meant "anointed with oil". Being anointed with oil was something that was associated with Kings and priests. Over time, the term "Messiah" came to have overtones of "divinely appointed Savior of the Israelite nation". The Messiah's coming was supposedly prophesied in Jewish scripture. The Messiah would be an all-conquering hero who would lead Israel out of a benighted state and into the light: freedom, world leadership, abundance, eternal earthly existence… and the list goes on.

The Greek word used to translate "Messiah" is "Christos". It too originally meant "anointed".

On his slow journey to Jerusalem, Jesus wrestles with a unique problem: *How can I get myself crucified?*

He did not foresee any problem about getting arrested. His mentor, John the Baptist, had been arrested when all he did was stay in the wilderness and preach and baptize and do spiritual work with his close disciples. Surely all Jesus had to do was turn up in Jerusalem and he would be arrested. The big problem was how to get crucified. As much as he had gotten up the noses of the religious authorities, he simply had not done anything that would see him nailed to a cross. Certainly the senior priests could collude with Herod and take him down the same route as John the Baptist: imprisonment and beheading. But to be actually crucified, Jesus would have to do something that upset not just the Jewish religious authorities but also the Romans.

A plan starts to take shape in Jesus's head. The initial genesis of the idea may have gone back to his conversation with the disciples:

> And he asked them, "But who do you say that I am?" Peter answered him, "You are the Messiah."
>
> - Mark 8:29

This is usually painted as being some magical insight that Peter had into the true nature of Jesus but the truth is Jesus totally ignores this suggestion. He then warns the disciples not to share the secret which he is about to tell them: that he has to suffer and die. Peter immediately takes Jesus aside and starts to rebuke him for suggesting this. Jesus turns on him and tells Peter off: "Get behind me, Satan!"

Peter – the one who is supposedly so insightful because he picked up that Jesus was the Jewish Messiah – is actually shown to be absolutely befuddled in his opinion about the nature of Jesus and his mission.

Consider this: If Jesus had not first asked what the disciples had thought of him but instead had revealed his second mission of suffering and dying, Peter would have never suggested he was the "Messiah". This is not what Messiahs do: they're supposed to be triumphal conquerors. No wonder Peter takes Jesus aside to rebuke him. Apart from anything else, he's just made Peter look stupid.

Albert Schweitzer, in *The Quest of the Historical Jesus*, tries to make the case that Jesus secretly believed he was the Messiah *but just a very different sort of Messiah* – one who wouldn't liberate Israel, one who wouldn't have any earthly power, one who wouldn't wage a military campaign and instead would die ignominiously on a cross. Ultimately, this is a line of argument that relies on Jesus being as befuddled as Peter. It is like arguing that Jesus thought: "I believe I am King but just a different sort of King – one who has absolutely no power, no throne, no subjects and no domain to rule." Jesus was simply too clear-minded for such contrarian logic. Jesus never even vaguely entertained the idea that he was the "Jewish Messiah".

First, because whatever reckoning of souls Jesus believed would happen was not aimed just at the oppressors of Israel. It was going to occur at least as much to Israelites.

Second, because the Jewish Messiah was supposed to save Israel as a whole. Jesus had no interest in this. He, like John the Baptist, was interested in individual Israelite souls and supporting their evolution. Both Jesus and John state that Israelite souls which have not borne fruit will be discarded (Luke 3:8-9; Matt 7:19). By contrast, the Jewish Messiah was supposed to rescue the whole nation of Israel.

Third, because the Jewish Messiah was supposed to restore the full glory of the old covenant: the Israelites would be led into a glorious new era where they would obey the Law and the Ten Commandments and God, in return, would make them great, glorious and gleeful. Jesus believed that the old covenant had been superseded.

Fourth, because Jesus simply had bigger fish to fry. He had a far, far bigger role to play than that which was ever envisioned for the Jewish "Messiah". Since the death of John the Baptist, he had become the central player in the evolution of God.

At the time when Peter makes the bizarre suggestion that Jesus is the Messiah, Jesus lets it go without comment. But as he heads towards Jerusalem, he starts to turn it over in his mind. It gives him an idea: if a disciple who really should know better is silly enough to believe he is the Messiah, then such a misperception could be his ticket to crucifixion. The Romans absolutely hated anyone who made the claim to be the Messiah. Like all occupiers of foreign lands, their primary worry was armed rebellion by the subjugated people. Amongst Israelites, anyone who wanted to lead an armed rebellion against Rome had to lay claim to being the liberating Messiah of legend. As soon as that claim was made, the Romans would rush any self-proclaimed Messiah onto a cross with all haste.[23]

All Jesus had to do then was to declare himself to be the Messiah, and, bang, the Roman authorities would be all over him and crucifying his ass. But Jesus was never going to say "I am the Messiah" because he would not lie about who he was. Saying that he was the "Messiah" would have made a mockery of his teachings which were all about laying up treasures in heaven and the individual evolution of individual souls. Like all mystics, he prized truth extraordinarily highly. He simply could not say he was the Jewish Messiah when he knew he wasn't. Far more important things were at hand... the kingdom of God was at hand.

What Jesus could do was use the clue that Peter had given him: people were prepared to think of him as the Messiah. Therefore, if he consciously imitated how a Messiah was supposed to behave, that would get him crucified.

This then is the Messianic secret: Jesus never for a heartbeat thought he was the Messiah. Anything that the Jewish Messiah was supposed to do was chickenfeed compared to the importance of what John the Baptist and Jesus did. But Jesus was prepared to ape the actions of the supposed Jewish Messiah in order to get himself crucified. He was prepared to imitate "Christ" – imitate "the Messiah".

It is for this reason that the only time we ever see anything vaguely resembling messianic behavior from Jesus is during and immediately after his entrance into Jerusalem.

Jesus had a further problem: while it was fine for him to be crucified, he was not prepared to have his disciples suffer the same agonizing fate.

It would be a delicate, tricky balancing act.

---

[23] Examples of Messiah claimants who were rapidly accelerated to their deaths by the Romans include Simon of Perae in 4 BC, Athronges around 2 BC and Judas of Galilee in 6 AD.

Behold the Kingly Messiah

In line with his determination to be arrested and crucified, Jesus does not enter Jerusalem quietly. He constructs a big entrance which will portray him in a kingly fashion. He organizes a colt to ride on and some of his followers to lay down palm leaves and coats for him to ride across. They call out: "Hosanna! Blessed is the one who comes in the name of the Lord! Blessed is the coming kingdom of our father David! Hosanna in the highest!" (Mark 11:9-10)

If Jesus's triumphal entrance into Jerusalem is historically correct, it has been very cleverly constructed by Jesus. First, it references Jewish scripture about a forthcoming king:

> Rejoice greatly, O daughter of Zion! Shout aloud, O daughter of Jerusalem! Behold, your king is coming to you; righteous and having salvation is he, humble and mounted on a donkey, on a colt, the foal of a donkey.
>
> - Zechariah 9:9

This Hollywood entrance, in itself, should give the authorities reason enough to seize him and crucify him. *I'm here. I'm making a claim for Kingship and Messiahship. Arrest me. Crucify me.*

But observe what is NOT shouted out: no-one shouts out "Messiah! Behold the Messiah!" Calling that out would have earmarked the followers as being part of a military-style brigade and they would have likely been rounded up as well. The more obscure and ambiguous "Hosanna!" (probably here meaning "Savior!") insulates them from such consequences.

(Indeed, the total lack of anyone calling out "Messiah!" during the procession is a strong indication that Peter's suggestion that Jesus was the Messiah was not only totally ignored by Jesus but also had no traction with the other disciples.)

So here Jesus is, entering in a kingly fashion, leading a crowd into Jerusalem and being feted as a savior. Surely that's enough to get him arrested and crucified. John the Baptist was arrested for less.

Jesus heads straight for the place where the Roman troops are supposed to be stationed: the Temple (Mark 11:11). He is making it as easy as possible for the Romans to arrest him.

But it is quiet. It's late. Nobody shows any interest in him. Possibly he had arrived too many days before the actual Passover and the Roman troops were not even there yet. He shrugs his shoulders and goes out to the nearby village of Bethany to stay at a follower's place.

Behold the Militant Messiah

Scriptures and folklore do not portray the predicted Jewish Messiah as a pacifist. He's not supposed to turn the other cheek as Jesus had recommended (Matt 5:38-39). He is supposed to be a military man leading an army of liberation. So Jesus comes up with a bold, outrageous tactic. One that will surely lead to his immediate arrest and crucifixion: he's going to trash the Temple. He will do the seemingly most out-of-character thing that he does in the entire Gospel: he will do something that looks violent.

The Temple in Jerusalem is huge. It is 1600 feet by 900 feet (500 by 275 meters). You could fit 25 American football fields into it.

This massive Temple has progressively exclusive areas.

First one enters the sprawling "Court of Gentiles": a huge market-style bazaar that is populated by money-changers, peddlers of souvenirs and sellers of animals for sacrifice. Anyone can enter it, even non-Jews.

Beyond that is "The Court of Women" into which only ritually clean male and female Israelites can enter.

Beyond that is "The Court of Israelites" into which only ritually clean Jewish men are permitted.

Beyond that is the "Court of Priests" forbidden to all but priests. It is there that the sacrifices of animals are made by the priests. To become a priest, you had to be born into the rabbinical class – you had to be a descendent of Aaron, the brother of Moses.

And beyond that was the "Holy of Holies": the supposed kingdom of God on earth, into which only the High Priest could go. He would walk into it once a year. Even then he would have a rope tied around his waist in case he died in there – that way other priests could haul him out without violating the Holy of Holies.

The whole Temple was constructed to reflect the Jewish religious hierarchy: at the very bottom were Gentiles and the unclean. Above them, Israelite women. Above them, Israelite men. Above them, the priests. At the very top of the pedestal, the High Priest.

This is the spiritual hierarchy that the teachings of John the Baptist and Jesus threw out the window.

Jesus did not believe in violence. He would not attack a person. That would be wrong. But he could make an attack on tables and coins and cages of animals. It is with this intent that he enters the Court of the Gentiles.

The Court of the Gentiles was the pivotal wheel in the huge money-making machine of the Temple. There people had to exchange their unclean foreign coins for righteous Temple currency – at an exchange rate dictated by the money-changers. Plus they needed to pay their half-shekel entry fee. Plus they had to buy the clean, spotless animals from the Court of the Gentiles to be offered up for sacrifice to God in the Court of Priests.

Jesus does not like the Temple. The sacrifices are pointless. The hierarchy is ridiculous.

> And they came to Jerusalem. And he entered the temple and began to drive out those who sold and those who bought in the temple, and he overturned the tables of the money-changers and the seats of those who sold pigeons. And he would not allow anyone to carry anything through the temple. And he was teaching them and saying to them, "Is it not written, 'My house shall be called a house of prayer for all the nations'? But you have made it a den of robbers."
>
> - Mark 11:15-17

The most amazing thing about this scene: Jesus did it solo!

Although "they" (Jesus and his followers) come into Jerusalem, Jesus alone enters the temple. A military leader would have had all his minions joining in. But Jesus does not want them to share his fate so he enters alone and executes his plan alone.

Surely this solo act of violence against the rip-offs of the religious hierarchy is enough to single him out for arrest and crucifixion.

Still the authorities do not arrest him.

The disturbance probably was not big enough to bother the Roman soldiers. The area was truly enormous. A disturbance in one tiny corner of it by one solitary man wasn't going to exactly bring the house down. Besides what did they care about Jews arguing amongst themselves? *Let the Jews sort out their own minor messes.* Moreover, the Romans knew that the Jews did not like Roman soldiers entering the Temple – especially near Passover.

Jesus overturns tables, scatters animals and money. He shouts a tirade against the greed of the Temple.

Nothing…

No arrest.

It must have been a shock to Jesus that he wasn't immediately arrested and slated for crucifixion.

So Jesus again leaves Jerusalem and again goes back to Bethany. Maybe the authorities just need time to get their act together. *What's a man got to do to get crucified around here?*

Slander

The next day Jesus comes back into Jerusalem. *I'm back. Arrest me.* Still the authorities do not move against him.

So Jesus starts preaching in a way geared to maximally upset the authorities.

If he can start to increase his following, surely that will force the hand of the authorities. And there are plenty of people around to listen to his preaching because it is the time of Passover. The city is starting to burst at the seams. It's not like there is TV or cinemas to distract the visitors. A preacher preaching outside the Temple is a major form of free entertainment… especially a preacher who is baiting the religious hierarchy.

And bait them he does. Jesus intimates that the high priests and elders are spiritually lower than tax collectors and prostitutes!

> "What do you think? A man had two sons. And he went to the first and said, 'Son, go and work in the vineyard today.' And he answered, 'I will not,' but afterward he changed his mind and went. And he went to the other son and said the same. And he answered, 'I go, sir,' but did not go. Which of the two did the will of his father?" They said, "The first." Jesus said to them, "Truly, I say to you, the tax collectors and the prostitutes go into the

kingdom of God before you. For John [the
Baptist] came to you in the way of righteousness,
and you did not believe him, but the tax collectors
and the prostitutes believed him. And even when
you saw it, you did not afterward change your
minds and believe him."

- Matthew 21:28-32

It doesn't get much more of a slap in the face than that.

This upstart country preacher also tells the parable of the vineyard
which is aimed at the high priests: they are the greedy tenants who are
supposed to be looking after the vineyard (the spiritual welfare of the
people) on God's behalf but they don't, they are only interested in their
own interests (Mark 12:1-12).

This *still* doesn't motivate the Jewish authorities enough to arrest
him.

Jesus decides to up the ante.

"Beware of the scribes, who like to walk around in
long robes and like greetings in the marketplaces
and have the best seats in the synagogues and the
places of honor at feasts, who devour widows'
houses and for a pretence make long prayers. They
will receive the greater condemnation."

- Mark, 12:38-40

Outright slander!

But even this isn't enough. No response from the authorities.
None.

Jesus begins to realize that, instead of forcing their hand, the
growing crowd of followers and listeners are forming a forbidding
hurdle to the religious authorities.

Then the chief priests, the teachers of the law and
the elders looked for a way to arrest him because
they knew he had spoken the parable against them.
But they were afraid of the crowd; so they left him
and went away.

- Mark 12:12 (NIV)

64

Jesus decides that he has to make it easy for them. He has to act. Time is running out. The period of the Passover will soon end, the pilgrims will start to disperse and the Roman troops will leave the capital. The opportunity for crucifixion is fading.[24]

Conspiracy

And so it is that Jesus secretly turns to his best and strongest disciple, the one that he trusts the most: the one he trusts with the money (John 13:29), a disciple so strong and independently-minded that he is prepared to question Jesus's judgment (John 12:3-5), the only disciple whom Jesus ever addresses as "Friend" (Matt 26:50), a disciple so close to Jesus that he leans on Jesus at the Last Supper and Jesus feeds him with his own hand (John 13:25-26), the only disciple where the bond of affection is so strong that a kiss between them is natural (Mark 14:45).

Judas. [25]

Jesus talks to Judas in private and tells him that he needs him to secretly go to the priesthood with an offer to betray Jesus in return for money. Judas must tell no-one else.

One can only imagine the desperate pleas Judas must have made to be spared this burden. But Judas does go to the priests. He agrees

---

[24] Amazingly, in neither the Gospels of Mark nor Luke does Jesus mention "the kingdom of God" in his public talks in Jerusalem. Was he worried that mentioning this would earmark not just himself but also his disciples as rebels and so place them in danger? Or did he feel he should not talk on it there because John the Baptist had given him the mission of taking the teachings about the kingdom of God into the villages and towns – not into Jerusalem? And so he didn't have the right to teach it there? Had the province of Jerusalem been given to a different student of John? A very interesting question.

[25] At that time, a kiss between members of the same sex was a common show of strong affection and it remains so in many countries. I once found myself abruptly kissed on the mouth in by a Russian man I had built up a great friendship with. Fortunately I knew it was the local way to show great affection and not a sexual gambit.

to "sell out" Jesus. In return for money, Judas tells the priests that he will deliver Jesus when he is away from crowds and followers. Part of the deal is that Jesus's followers are to be left alone. The priests solemnly promise that only Jesus will be arrested. And indeed, they stick to that promise. At Jesus's arrest, one of his followers strikes out with a sword and cuts off the ear of the servant of the high priest but, amazingly, is not arrested (Mark 14:47).

Plus there is a very big bonus that Judas gives the priests: he feeds them grounds for crucifying Jesus. Judas tells them that Jesus preaches about "the kingdom of God".

Aha! A kingdom! The Romans will hate the idea of a Jew promoting the coming of a kingdom separate from Roman rule. That's insurrectionist language.

So the conspiracy is put on track with Jesus's own hidden hand on the tiller.

The Gospels are very plain that Jesus knew what Judas was going to do. If he had not wanted it to happen, he could have stopped it. At the last supper, Jesus turns to Judas:

> Jesus said to him [Judas], "What you are going to do, do quickly." Now no one at the table knew why he said this to him.
>
> - John 13: 27-28.

There are only two possibilities:
1. Jesus was psychic and psychically knew that Judas was going to betray him... but, nevertheless, let it happen; or
2. Jesus knew because he had instructed Judas as to what he required to be done.

Which do you think is the more likely?

Neither Judas nor Jesus tells the others because the rest of the disciples would have tried to stop it happening.

Judas had his own terrible cross to bear. He knew that the other disciples would never believe that he had betrayed Jesus at the behest of Jesus. He would be forever an outcast. But such was the strength of his love for his teacher that he accepted his pivotal role in the divine drama.

I invite you to go back over the scenes with Judas and realize the poignant sadness of two great friends who loved each other saying goodbye: Judas leaning on Jesus at the supper… Jesus feeding Judas out of his own hand.

A final symbol: The Last Supper

In the hours leading up to his death, Jesus shares a final meal with his inner sanctum. The great mystic teacher gives his disciples two last symbols: one they clearly understood and one they may not have understood so well.

Jesus takes bread in his hands. Every disciple there knows that bread is one of their teacher's favorite images for the transformed soul – the flour that has been raised up by the leaven symbolizing the soul that has been raised up by union with the Holy Spirit. Even though this bread is unleavened because it is the Passover, Jesus still uses it as a symbol of a Son of Man: "Take; this is my body." (Mark 14:22). It is symbolic of what each disciple needs to realize inside themselves: a transformed, baptized-by-spirit soul inside their physical body.

Then he gives them a symbol for what is to come.

> And he took a cup, and when he had given thanks
> he gave it to them, and they all drank of it. And he
> said to them, "This is my blood of the covenant,
> which is poured out for many."
>
> - Mark 14:23-24.

So it is that blood was the symbol of the sealing of the New Covenant – just as blood had been the symbol of the sealing of the Old Covenant of Moses. Under the New Covenant, man would transform his soul: his soul would be baptized-by-Spirit and so enter into the domain of God. Via the transformed soul of Jesus, God would experience an ultimate in human suffering and become capable of compassion and so act to wipe out the hopeless and evil souls.

But, within 24 hours, the New Covenant would be broken.

The Arrest

Not long after sending Judas off on his secret mission, Jesus departed for the Mount of Olives and the Garden of Gethsemane with just a handful of disciples.

How did Judas, who had already left, know where Jesus would be?

Because it had been pre-arranged between the two of them.

It would be made as easy as possible for the authorities: only Jesus and a tiny number of disciples would be there. It was planned as bloodless. It would only involve the arrest of Jesus alone and not any of his followers. Jesus's party took only two swords with them – Jesus saying, "It is enough" (Luke 22:38). Why would Jesus go into a remote, quiet garden with a tiny number of followers and only two miserable swords when he was in danger of being arrested? There is only one logical answer: because he wanted to be arrested, because he planned to be arrested. Two swords were never going to be enough to stop him being arrested – but they may be of some help in assisting his followers to beat a hasty retreat and run away. The protection of his disciples is as important to Jesus as fulfilling God's will that he be crucified.

Now that the moment is closing in on him, Jesus feels the gut-wrenching fear of the pain to come. Previously he has been able to focus on the challenge of getting himself arrested and crucified. But now that this has been arranged, his thoughts turn to the horrifying reality of what that means.

Like any mystic, death does not worry him but the hours – perhaps days – of searing agony – that is something no sane person invites. Jesus prostrates himself on the ground and pleads with God:

> "Abba[26], Father, all things are possible for you.
> Remove this cup from me. Yet not what I will, but
> what you will."
>
> - Mark 14:36.

But he receives no release from his mission.

Jesus finishes praying.

As they still haven't come to arrest him, Jesus goes back to prayer again.

Still no arrest.

So he goes back to pray a third time.

At length, a group of men sent by the priests come with swords

---

[26] Aramaic for "father".

and clubs to arrest Jesus, guided by Judas.

Judas cleverly creates one last moment with his beloved friend and teacher (rabbi). Judas could have hidden behind a bush in the dark and just pointed Jesus out – that would have been the safe thing to do. *"He's the one over there by himself praying."* Then the other disciples would have never known for sure that Judas was the "betrayer". But he wants one last moment with his cherished friend. Plus, in standing next to Jesus, Judas has a chance to shield him if anything goes wrong.

Judas cautions the arresting party not to hurt his friend and teacher: "The one I will kiss is the man. Seize him and lead him away safely." (Mark 14:44; ISV)

And so Judas creates one last precious human moment before the humiliation and pain to come. "…he went up to him at once and said, 'Rabbi!' And he kissed him." (Mark 14:45)

A moment of stillness frozen in time between the two great friends which would, for two thousand years, be wrongly interpreted as a betrayal.

In this slender moment in time, Jesus sees only Judas. He has not yet sighted the gang sent to arrest him. He looks at Judas and calls him Friend/Comrade. "Friend, do what you came to do." (Matt 26:50).

And then the humiliation and pain start. "And they laid hands on him and seized him" (Mark 14:46). As it is happening, you can almost hear Jesus say, *"Finally!"*

> "Have you come out with swords and clubs to arrest me as though I were a bandit? Day after day I was with you in the temple teaching, and you did not arrest me."
>
> - Mark:14:48-49 (ISV).

The Trial of Jesus

We have to regard the Gospels' accounts of the trial of Jesus and the words exchanged between Jesus and the priests and Pilate as fanciful if only because, well, who was there to hear them?

Of course, it may well be that some things which the Gospels allege Jesus said at his trial were said at an earlier time by Jesus. For instance, take this example of an alleged interchange between Pilate and Jesus from the Gospel of John:

> So Pilate entered his headquarters again and called Jesus and said to him, "Are you the King of the Jews?" Jesus answered, "Do you say this of your own accord, or did others say it to you about me?" Pilate answered, "Am I a Jew? Your own nation and the chief priests have delivered you over to me. What have you done?" Jesus answered, "My kingdom is not of this world. If my kingdom were of this world, my servants would have been fighting, that I might not be delivered over to the Jews. But my kingdom is not from the world."
>
> - John 18:33-37

It is quite believable that at some stage in his ministry Jesus did say: "My kingdom is not of this world". What is virtually impossible to believe is that there was anyone around to hear a conversation between Jesus and Pilate. It is also impossible to believe that the notoriously ruthless Pilate would spend that much time talking to a despised Jew.

Things we can have some level of confidence in:

- Jesus was arrested at night and crucified the very next day. Jesus had a growing band of followers so authorities wouldn't want to muck around and give his followers time to re-group and stage protests.
- It was likely a three-stage process:
    1. An interview during the night by a kangaroo court of priests. They decide that this annoying country bumpkin preacher needs to go.
    2. A meeting of the Sanhedrin (the Jewish religious high council) is hurriedly convened first thing the next day which signs off on Jesus being guilty under Jewish Law.
    3. There is a sign-off from the Roman authorities (i.e., Pontius Pilate) to crucify him under Roman jurisdiction.
- It is unlikely that Pontius Pilate had much if any of a conversation with Jesus. He may have had a perfunctory conversation which is what is recorded in the Gospel of Mark. But the extended conversation as recorded in the Gospel of John is extraordinarily fanciful. Pilate was a brutal man. He crucified thousands of Jews. A few years later, in 37

AD, there was a revolt by Samaritans. Pilate's put-down of this revolt was so vicious that even the Romans didn't like it and he was sacked and recalled to Rome. What would Pilate have cared about the crucifixion of one Jew, more or less? Whether Jesus was guilty or not, Passover was a good time to make an example of someone by crucifying a potential troublemaker.

Though highly questionable, we are nevertheless going to have a look at the account of Jesus's trial as found in the Gospel of Mark. It is the most minimalist account in the Bible.

> And they led Jesus to the high priest. And all the chief priests and the elders and the scribes came together... Now the chief priests and the whole Council were seeking testimony against Jesus to put him to death, but they found none. For many bore false witness against him, but their testimony did not agree. And some stood up and bore false witness against him, saying, "We heard him say, 'I will destroy this temple that is made with hands, and in three days I will build another, not made with hands.'" Yet even about this their testimony did not agree.
>
> - Mark 14:53-59

It is no wonder that their testimony didn't agree because, at least in the Gospel of Mark, Jesus did not say that. The actual conversation went like this:

> And as he came out of the temple, one of his disciples said to him, "Look, Teacher, what wonderful stones and what wonderful buildings!" And Jesus said to him, "Do you see these great buildings? There will not be left here one stone upon another that will not be thrown down."
>
> - Mark 13:1-2

There is no mention of Jesus rebuilding the temple in three days. This conversation is simply Jesus, the mystic teacher, pointing out the ephemeral nature of the physical compared to the spiritual. The Temple is, far and away, the most impressive building the disciples have ever seen but, like all physical reality, it's transitory. It could also have a religious implication: Jesus knew that the New Covenant spelt the end of the old ways of religion as instantiated in the Temple.

Back to the trial of Jesus...

> And the high priest stood up in the midst and asked Jesus, "Have you no answer to make? What is it that these men testify against you?" But he remained silent and made no answer. Again the high priest asked him, "Are you the Messiah, the Son of the Blessed?"
>
> - Mark 14:60-61.

And Jesus answers them: "You say that I am." (Luke 22:70[27])

> And the high priest tore his garments and said, "What further witnesses do we need? You have heard his blasphemy. What is your decision?" And they all condemned him as deserving death. And some began to spit on him and to cover his face and to strike him, saying to him, "Prophesy!" And the guards received him with blows...
> And as soon as it was morning, the chief priests held a consultation with the elders and scribes and the whole Council.
>
> - Mark 15:63-65; 16:1

---

[27] I have used the reply from the Gospel of Luke which is absolutely coherent with the reply in the Gospel of Matthew which is "You have said so" (26:64). The reply in the Gospel of Mark is "I am..." (14:26). Both Matthew and Luke had access to far more pristine versions of Mark than we do now and they agree on this much vaguer reply by Jesus. Because of this, the likelihood is that the original version of Mark was something like "You say that I am" but was subsequently altered by a later scribe to "I am" (either willfully or accidentally). It is this altered version that has been handed down to contemporary times. Hence, my favoring of the Luke version here.

What is most interesting about this Jewish inquisition of Jesus is that it had absolutely nothing to do with why he was crucified. The Romans would not have crucified him for having spiritual beliefs or for supposed blaspheming against Jewish canon. The things that made the priests furious at Jesus – like slandering their greed and telling them that prostitutes were more spiritually advanced than they were, or even allowing that he might be the "Son of the Blessed" – these things were not crucifiable offenses. And the high priests knew that. Instead they would have to make the case that Jesus was guilty of sedition: that he was an insurrectionist preaching against Rome and its power. They had already tried to trap him into speaking against Rome while he had been preaching in Jerusalem.

> And they sent to him some of the Pharisees and some of the Herodians, to trap him in his talk... "Is it lawful to pay taxes to Caesar, or not? Should we pay them, or should we not?"
>
> - Mark 12:13-14

But Jesus had turned this into a joke:

> "Bring me a denarius and let me look at it." And they brought one. And he said to them, "Whose likeness and inscription is this?" They said to him, "Caesar's." Jesus said to them, "Render to Caesar the things that are Caesar's, and to God the things that are God's."
>
> - Mark 12:15-17

You can almost hear the disciples laughing in the background at this zinger.

To get Jesus crucified, the high priests could not present him as a blasphemer. They had to present him as guilty of sedition – trying to undermine the rule of Rome. They had six things going in their favor:

1. It is almost certain that they had done this sort of thing already: wanted someone dead whom they did not have the power to kill and found a way to present the matter to the Romans in such a way that they would rubberstamp the execution.

2. Jesus had already demonstrated an unwillingness to defend himself against charges.
3. Jesus had built up something of a following and occupying forces hate leaders with followings.
4. It was the Passover and the Romans were twitchy about disturbances at this time of year. Even if Jesus wasn't guilty, the example of crucifying someone was useful for discouraging others.
5. Pontius Pilate was a ruthless governor and would not have been fussy about evidence.
6. Jesus has been consistently preaching about the coming of a "kingdom of God". The high priests could make that sound like he was trying to stir up an insurrection against Rome whereby it would be replaced by a kingdom of God with Jesus himself as King – a title that Jesus never so much as ever mentioned.

The high priests most probably had no inkling of what Jesus meant by "the kingdom of God". To them, it was a very useful phrase to latch onto for mounting a case against Jesus under the charge of sedition. That is obviously what Pilate thinks the charge is.

> And they bound Jesus and led him away and delivered him over to Pilate. And Pilate asked him, "Are you the King of the Jews?" And he answered him, "You have said so." And the chief priests accused him of many things. And Pilate again asked him, "Have you no answer to make? See how many charges they bring against you." But Jesus made no further answer...
>
> - Mark 15:1-5

Pilate would not have spent much time with Jesus (if any). His name is entered into the book for crucifixion and he is passed over to the soldiers who do what they do to anyone who has pretensions of challenging the power of Rome: they scourge him and beat him up. One of them gets creative in their sarcasm and weaves a crown from thorn branches – a sadistic parody of the Roman civic crown made of oak leaves. It is crushed onto Jesus's head and blood flows from where the thorns pierce his scalp.

Jesus takes it stoically. This was the fate he had planned to happen. That same morning, he is rushed off to his death.

It has only been a matter of hours since he was arrested but when Jesus emerges again in public, he is a very different man. He is bloodied and bruised. He has been beaten, viciously scourged, spat upon, and a sarcastic crown of thorns has been crushed into his head.

As with all condemned prisoners of the day, he has the crossbeam of the cross lashed to his scourged shoulders and he is forced to haul it out through the gates of Jerusalem and up a hill to the place of crucifixion, Golgotha, the place of the skull.

The Bible records him as so weakened that someone in the crowd had to help him with the Cross.

If he had had the strength to look around for his followers, he would have seen none. They were too frightened to be seen, too scared of being arrested and sharing his fate. Only at Golgotha do some of his female followers steal in to watch Jesus's crucifixion from a distance. These women would have seen Jesus's bloodied clothes ripped from him. They would have heard the blows of the hammer as the nails were driven through his flesh. As they were at a distance, the women would have seen the blows of the hammer fractionally before the sounds of hammer hitting nail reached them. Later, when Jesus screamed out four Aramaic words near his death, they would hear those too.

The women saw his bloodied, naked body hauled up to vertical.

This was it. This was the second mission. The divine mission.

This was what God the Father had asked of Jesus. This was what God needed from him.

And God was with Jesus every step of this painful way – suffering and bleeding with him. God felt the scourging, the crush of the crown of thorns, the agony of the nails driven through the flesh, the loneliness, the humiliation, the injustice of it all, the first terrible wrench as Jesus's body is hauled onto the Cross. For God needed the Passion of the Christ to learn what it is like to suffer, what it is like to endure the lot of Humankind. And Jesus, surrendering to his divine mission, was providing suffering for God in abundance.

But what is this thing we call "God"?

Jesus Delusion III

The Jews bear all the blame for the crucifixion of Jesus

Despite the Romans being the ones driving the nails into Jesus's flesh, a couple of the Gospels squarely point the finger at the Jews as bearing all responsibility for the crucifixion.

> So when Pilate saw that he was gaining nothing, but rather that a riot was beginning, he took water and washed his hands before the crowd, saying, "I am innocent of this man's blood; see to it yourselves." And all the people answered, "His blood be on us and on our children!"
>
> - Matthew 27:24-25

Over the next two millennia, this and other Gospel passages would lead to the sometimes horrific persecution of Jews. Yet the truth is that Jesus was a Jew. The post-crucifixion Jesus movement started as a sect within Judaism. Christianity was pioneered and spread by Jews.

The faith-based Christian view of the Passion of the Christ is that God required Jesus to be crucified to expiate the sins of humankind. All Jesus had to do was turn up in Jerusalem, as God had arranged the whole grisly business for his Son in advance.

In contrast, the Passion of the Christ portrayed in this book can be summed up by: "God has no other hands than yours". Jesus was called upon to be crucified but it was up to him to heed the call of God and make it happen.

Under either of these pictures, there is a pretty obvious conclusion as to who is ultimately responsible for the crucifixion of Jesus.

God.

In the Garden of Gethsemane, Jesus begged Abba – God the Father – to release him from this cross that was almost impossible to bear.

But God would not let him off the hook.

But what is this thing we call "God"?

76

The crucifixion is an embarrassing failure

There are those who regard Jesus's crucifixion as an embarrassing failure. But how can something be a failure if it was what you were planning to happen? The crucifixion is actually a massive triumph of human will. If you do not see the glory in Jesus's submission to crucifixion, then you do not understand the first thing about Jesus. It was a triumph of unbelievable humility. *In the end, my pain doesn't matter. The advancement of the divine is what matters.*

It was also an act of unbelievable love for humanity. Jesus absolutely believed that God experiencing suffering via him would bring about a close understanding of God for suffering humanity. This could result in only good things for humankind.

There is little doubt that many of the early Jesus-followers were embarrassed by the whole crucifixion thing. *How can anyone be convinced to believe in a divine master who was killed like a common criminal?* This is probably the provocation for selling delusions like Jesus had to die in agony to expiate our sins. And delusions like Jesus was born the son of God. And delusions like the idea that the crucifixion was necessary so that he could rise again on the third day and conquer death, prove his divinity and become the Savior of souls.

The crucifixion was no failure. It was one of the great triumphs of the human spirit. It was one man stepping up to a very big plate and agreeing to be the conduit for the education of God.

But what is this thing we call "God"?

Jesus Delusion V

The God Delusions

Tied up with many Jesus Delusions are very delusory ideas about God.

Scratch the surface of most faith-based Christians and you are going to find that, ultimately, their idea of God is a giant Zeus-like father-figure up in the sky/heaven, complete with throne, radiating light, compassion, goodness, etc.

There couldn't be a more delusory idea about God. This is man making God in his own image.

> But some people want to see God with their eyes
> as they see a cow.
>
> - Meister Eckhart, *Complete Mystical Works* 14 (b), p. 117.

> If we want to search for God, we shall look within ourselves because on the outside we will never find HIM.
>
> - Paracelsus

Part III

A short history of God

Then Moses said to God, "If I come to the people of Israel and say to them, 'The God of your fathers has sent me to you,' and they ask me, 'What is his name?' what shall I say to them?" God said to Moses, "I AM THAT I AM." And he said, "Say this to the people of Israel, 'I AM has sent me to you.'"

- Exodus 3:13-14.

In the Being...

In the beginning of all things, there was not even God.
And also there was not nothing.
In the beginning, there is just Being, Isness, Existence, Beingness.
Isness is all that there IS.

> In the beginning was only Being,
> One without a second.
>
> — Chandogya Upanishad VI, 2.2, p.183.

> Being is the particular property of God... Being is
> the first name. Everything that is deficient is
> descent from being.
>
> — Meister Eckhart, *Selected Writings*,
> p.166.

> Jesus said, "If they say to you, 'Where have you
> come from?' say to them, 'We have come from the
> light, from the place where the light came into
> being by itself…'"
>
> — Gospel of Thomas 50

> Prior to Creation, there was only the infinite or Ein
> Sof filling all existence.
>
> — Isaac Luria, Etz Chaim, Arizal,
> Heichal A'K, anaf

> Before He gave any shape to the world, before He
> produced any form, He was alone, without form
> and without resemblance to anything else.
>
> — *Zohar*, part ii, section 'Bo' 42b

If you are now thinking, *"No, before there was being, there MUST have been nothing."*, see Appendix Five: Something on Nothing.

The Evolution of Essence

But Beingness does not sit still as there is nothing to contain it. It spreads. It mingles with itself. It reacts with itself.

In so mingling, Beingness goes beyond just being Being.

Beingness merges into beingness and, in so merging, expands itself which is the Essence of Love.

Beingness surrenders itself unto itself which is the Essence of Peace.

Beingness touches itself and asks, "What is this?" which is the Essence of Curiosity.

Beingness recognizes itself which is the Essence of Consciousness.

Beingness acts upon itself which is the Essence of Will.

Beingness recognizes itself as itself. "Ah, this is me." Which is the Essence of Truth.

> There is an uncreated Spirit and a created Spirit which flows from the uncreated Spirit... The uncreated spirit is eternal being.
>
> - Meister Eckhart, *Selected Writings*, p.239.

> The masters make a distinction between being and essence. Where being is active being in the Father, it is also essence.
>
> - Meister Eckhart, *Selected Writings*, p.247.[28]

The Godhead

And so it is that Beingness evolved into a great spiritual field – a field capable of feeling, willing.

Mystics sometimes refer to this field as "the Godhead".

---

[28] Here Eckhart seems to be referring to Thomas Aquinas – and presumably others. See *Summa Theologiae* I, Question 3, Article 4 where Aquinas discusses whether Essence and Existence are the same in God.

God and Godhead are as far apart from each other
as heaven and earth...

All that is in the Godhead is One, and of this no
one can speak. God acts, while the Godhead does
not act.

> - Meister Eckhart, *Selected Writings*,
> pp.233, 234.

The birth of the physical universe

In its first attempt to understand what it was, the Godhead wills
energy out of itself.

This super-concentrated pin-prick of energy explodes.

The physical universe is begun.

The Big Bang.

And that energy starts to evolve.

> The deathless Self meditated upon
> Himself and projected the universe
> As evolutionary energy.
>
> > - Mundaka Upanishad II, 1:8, p.110.

Prior to Creation, there was only the infinite Or
Ein Sof filling all existence. When it arose in God's
Will to create worlds and emanate the
emanated...He contracted [in Hebrew "*tzimtzum*"]
Himself in the point at the center, in the very
center of His light. He restricted that light,
distancing it to the sides surrounding the central
point, so that there remained a void, a hollow
empty space, away from the central point... After
this tzimtzum... He drew down from the Or Ein
Sof a single straight line [of light] from His light
surrounding [the void] from above to below [into
the void], and it chained down descending into
that void...

In the space of that void He emanated, created, formed and made all the worlds.

- Isaac Luria, Etz Chaim, Arizal, Heichal A'K, anaf 2

What am I?

The Godhead meditated upon itself.

It came to a realization: *It did not know what It was.*

I AM did not know what it was.

How do YOU know what YOU are?

You look in the mirror. You look at your body. You see yourself reflected in the eyes and opinions of others.

But, if you are everything, you cannot see yourself in a mirror. You cannot see yourself reflected in the eyes of another because there is no other.

How could the Godhead know what it was?

It could only do this by dividing, by spawning parts of itself, by giving birth to parts of itself.

So the Godhead contracted unto itself… But it could not contract ALL of itself. There still had to be a spiritual field left. There had to be some uncontracted spiritual field on which the rest of the Godhead could contract and onto which it could spawn tiny parts of itself.

After contracting as tight as it could, the condensed part of the Godhead then broke its boundaries and spawned out tiny droplets of itself onto the remaining spiritual field.

The spiritual field still ran through these droplets, but it was not the droplets.

These droplets, these tiny slices of the contracted Godhead, were the souls.

Many many billions of them.

Each one as individual as a snowflake from a snow cloud.

And so it is that at the very core of your being, you are unique… and you are a Son of God.

We do not know what God is. God Himself does not know what He is…

- John Scotus Erigena

God wished to behold God.

> - Kabbalah oral tradition

Imperishable is the Lord of Love.
As from a blazing fire thousands of sparks
Leap forth, so millions of beings arise
From the Lord of Love…

> - Mundaka Upanishad II, 1

Congratulations to those who are alone and chosen, for you will find the kingdom. For you have come from it, and you will return there again.

> - Jesus, Gospel of Thomas 49

When God created heaven and earth and all creatures, God did not act. There was no work for him to do, and there was no action or work in him. Then God said: "We will make a likeness" (*Genesis* 1:26). It is easy to create something: we do this as and when we will. But what I make, I make alone, with myself and in myself and I impress my own image fully upon it... When God made humankind, he performed in the soul a work that was like himself...

> - Meister Eckhart, *Selected Writings,* p.232.

The Trinity

After this divine spawning, there was a trinity of spiritual entities:
1. The souls
2. The uncontracted universal spiritual field (the uncontracted Godhead) onto which the rest of the Godhead had condensed and onto which it had spawned the souls. This uncontracted Godhead is the Holy Spirit/Brahman/the One.
3. That which remained of the condensed Godhead after the spawning of the Souls. This is what we have come to know as

"God" – what Jesus called "God the Father" because it had fathered the souls.

By giving birth to the souls, God had been born.

> The god of creation, Brahma
> Born of the Godhead through meditation
>> - Katha Upanishad II, 1:6, p.91.

> From infinite Godhead came forth Brahma
>> - Mundaka Upanishad I, 1:1, p.109.

> Brahman brought the Lord out of himself;
> Therefore he is called the Self-existent.
>> - Taittiriya Upanishad II, 7:1, p.144.

> But when I emerged by free choice and received
> my created being, I came into the possession of a
> God for, until creatures came into existence, God
> was not "God", but was rather what he was.
>> - Meister Eckhart, *Selected Writings,*
>> pp.204-5.

The Holy Spirit/Brahman/The One

Just as physical objects exist in and on space-time, so too do spiritual entities exist in and on the Holy Spirit/the One.

When a soul purifies itself enough and fuses with the One/Holy Spirit, it is fusing with the original – if diluted – Godhead.

St Teresa of Avila described it as "…celestial union with the uncreated Spirit". (*The Interior Castle*, "The Seventh Mansions" II:9.)

> …God's ground and the soul's ground are one ground.
>> - Meister Eckhart, *Complete Mystical Works of Meister Eckhart*, Sermon 51, p.273.

> And it happened that when the Lord came up out
> of the water, the whole fountain of the holy spirit
> came down on him and rested on him. It said to
> him "My Son, I was waiting for you in all the
> prophets, waiting for you to come so I could rest
> in you…"
>
> > - The Gospel of the Hebrews, see
> > Robert J. Miller (ed), *The Complete
> > Gospels*, p. 432.

> As pure water poured into pure water
> Becomes the very same, so does the Self
> Of the illumined man or woman, Nachiketa,
> Verily become one with the Godhead
>
> > - Katha Upanishad II, 1:15, p.92.

Jesus did not become a Son of God through baptism by the Holy Spirit. He was already that. He became a Son of the Holy Spirit through baptism by the Holy Spirit.

The birth trauma of the souls

The idea that the Godhead could know itself by spawning parts of itself turned out to have been doomed before it started.

You are either all-powerful, invulnerable, boundless or you are not; instead you are weak, vulnerable, bounded. In being ejaculated from the unbounded, the souls went into traumatized shock.

Imagine you were yanked from the comforting arms of your beloved into being crushed between two beds of nails. Then you would have some small inkling of the birth traumas of the souls. As the souls have no sense of time, this insane moment of their birth does not seem like some short event – it seems almost infinite in length.

Every soul was traumatized by its ejection from the condensed Godhead. At the deepest depths of your soul, you are traumatized and have been since the instant of divine separation.

Look around.

Does this world look like a world populated by souls that are divine slices of pure Godhead? Or does it resemble more a lunatic asylum for souls traumatized since the birth of time?

We have seen that mystic after mystic says that the soul has to be made pure, into what it was before it was born.

It has to turn its energies back to what they were at the very beginning... before it was even born.

The ancient mystics talk in terms of "purification".

In modern terms, we would say "detraumatization".

In the end there can only be one reason for this: the birth trauma of the souls.

Moreover, this gives us a solution to the age-old Problem of Evil. How is it that the soul is capable of such evil even though it came from the purely divine? The answer lies in the birth trauma of the souls.

The Fall

God the Father was now surrounded by tiny slices of itself: snowdrops from the vast cloud of Being.

But they were not the tiny mirrors of himself that he had expected. They were distorted and traumatized.

We must presume that the souls carried on like traumatized humans do: shock, complaints, blaming, violence. God did not know what to make of the psychotic behavior of souls, but one thing he was sure of: *He was not like that.*

And he was right. He was not like that because he had not gone through the birth trauma of the souls. This was the start of God's self-opinion. *I might not know what I am but I know what I am not, and I'm not like that.*

Disgusted, he kicked the souls out of his presence.

Expunged them.

Ejected them.

The Fall...

Incarnation

Ejected from nearness to God, the souls plunge through the vibrations and bottom out at a vibration close to the physical plane.

As traumatized as they were, the souls nevertheless contained a slice of divine Will. And some sought to exercise that Will.

Looking through the vibrations, they could sense the physical plane that had evolved... the plants... the beasts.

And they realized that they could attach themselves to the most advanced of these animals and so exercise their slice of divine will via the bodies of these animals.

And so it was that they started to attach themselves to the most advanced creatures on the planet: naked apes.

(There is a very specific and startling implication from this. See Appendix Six: An historical implication.)

The first mystic

For many thousands of earthly years, God the Father had no interest in his progeny – those pathetic souls he had ejected from his presence. But then the earliest of mystics started to do inner work. They started to purify their souls.

Somewhere, sometime, someone became the first person to fuse their soul with spirit. He or she had so purified their soul that the Holy Spirit could enter into it and the two could fuse. This was something that could not escape God's attention. *Hello, there's been a disturbance in the force.*

God turned his attention to the world of incarnated souls.

And was amazed.

Stunned.

These pathetic rejects had become something.

They had attached themselves to ape bodies and had pulled that species up from the evolutionary gutter. They had started villages and farms and cities. They had laws and rituals and codes and language and writing and morality.

They had changed.

They had evolved.

The fact that they evolved at all was staggering.

These were the slices of Himself that He Himself had rejected.

How could they have changed and evolved?

He Himself had not changed, not evolved. He was exactly the same as when he had ejected the souls from his presence.

These incarnated souls even had a belief in superior spiritual entities – gods.

Staggering.

And there was one particular tribe that showed a promising potential to believe not just in a pantheon of "gods" but in just one God.

So God focused his attention on this one tribe…

The Job Intersection

Whilst examining the tribe of the Israelites, God was confronted by a startling realization: he did not understand Man.

This is what is recorded in the Book of Job, one of the most striking meditations ever on the relationship of the human with the divine. In this book, Job becomes a plaything of God and Satan.

Job starts off as a favorite of God: "Have you considered my servant Job, that there is none like him on the earth, a blameless and upright man, who fears God and turns away from evil?" (Job 1:8)

But Satan tells God that this is just because Job has had it easy and God has "…blessed the work of his hands, and his possessions have increased in the land" (Job 1:10).

So God bets Satan that Satan can't turn Job against God. God will lose this bet.

In one day, Satan kills off all of Job's children and all Job's possessions are expunged but this isn't enough to turn Job against God. "Naked I came from my mother's womb, and naked shall I return. The Lord gave, and the Lord has taken away; blessed be the name of the Lord." (Job 1:21).

So then Satan turns his attention to Job's flesh and the entirety of Job's body is covered in loathsome sores from the top of his head to the soles of his feet. Still, Job does not turn against God. (Hence the expression "the patience of Job"). "Shall we receive good from God, and shall we not receive evil?" (Job 2:10)

But, after seven days and nights of this never-ceasing grinding torment, Job loses it. He's had 168 tortured hours to contemplate his life and the state of the world and he doesn't like what he sees. He turns on God and attacks him for failing to understand or care about human suffering: "He destroys both the blameless and the wicked. When disaster brings sudden death, he mocks at the calamity of the innocent. The earth is given into the hand of the wicked; he covers the faces of its judges – if it is not he, who then is it?"

Job even directs his words of judgment at God himself: "Does it seem good to you to oppress, to despise the work of your hands and favor the designs of the wicked? Have you eyes of flesh? Do you see as man sees?" (Job 9:22-24; 10:3-4)

Consider how extraordinary this passage is. Man, in the person of Job, has developed a sense of morality so strong that he believes that even God should be subject to it – and God does not measure up.

Job's friends lounge around and tell him not to be so stupid, that God is by definition just and therefore Job must deserve what he's getting: "Know then that God exacts of you less than your guilt deserves." (Job 11:6)

Job is having none of that nonsense. "You whitewash with lies. Worthless physicians are you all… Will you speak falsely for God and speak deceitfully for him?" (Job 13:4,7)

Job's withering critique eventually provokes God himself to appear in a whirlwind and threaten Job with divine fury: "Gird up your loins like a man. I will question you, and you make it known to me. Will you even put me in the wrong? Will you condemn me that you may be in the right? Have you an arm like God, and can you thunder with a voice like his?" (Job 40:7-9)

Job, fearing for his life, covers his mouth.

Eventually God calms down and, in the most extraordinary moment in the Old Testament, God concedes that Job was right!

The friends who defended God's character are adjudged to be totally in the wrong and God speaks to them in contained fury: "My anger burns against you… for you have not spoken of me what is right, as my servant Job has. Now therefore take seven bulls and seven rams and go to my servant Job and offer up a burnt offering for yourselves. And my servant Job shall pray for you, for I will accept his prayer not to deal with you according to your folly. For you have not spoken of me what is right, as my servant Job has." (Job 42:7-8)

!

God has conceded that Job was in the right: God does not understand human suffering and the lot of humankind. These pathetic rejects had evolved into something beyond God's power to comprehend. He does not understand courage and compassion, morality and kindness, frustration and fortitude.

God has not eyes of flesh so he cannot understand humanity.

God formed a determination – the strangest determination in the history of existence: that he would come to experience as humanity experiences. He would come to see with eyes of flesh, feel as a man feels and so experience the defining experience of human life: unjustified suffering.

And there was a way he could do it too: via the Holy Spirit. The Holy Spirit could connect Him to a transformed, baptized-by-spirit soul. Any person who has had their soul baptized-by-Spirit had entered the kingdom of God. Their soul is now a domain which God can connect to – via which He can feel as a man or woman feels.

He just needed an Israelite to transform their soul – to have it baptized by Spirit.

Enter John the Baptist.

Enter one of his star pupils, Yeshua – whom we remember as "Jesus".

God at the Christ Intersection

After many millennia of neglect, God had drawn near to humanity.

"The time is fulfilled, and the kingdom of God is
at hand…"

- Mark 1:15

God had come back to the rejected souls looking for them to do for Him the one thing that He Himself could not do: **Evolve**.

God came back looking to harvest the fruits of the journey of the souls despite having rejected and neglected these very same souls. And Jesus told a parable to very clearly illustrate this exact point:

For it will be like a man going on a journey, who
called his servants and entrusted to them his
property. To one he gave five talents, to another
two, to another one, to each according to his
ability. Then he went away. He who had received
the five talents went at once and traded with them,

and he made five talents more. So also he who had the two talents made two talents more. But he who had received the one talent went and dug in the ground and hid his master's money. Now after a long time the master of those servants came and settled accounts with them. And he who had received the five talents came forward, bringing five talents more, saying, "Master, you delivered to me five talents; here I have made five talents more." His master said to him, "Well done, good and faithful servant. You have been faithful over a little; I will set you over much. Enter into the joy of your master." And he also who had the two talents came forward, saying, "Master, you delivered to me two talents; here I have made two talents more." His master said to him, "Well done, good and faithful servant. You have been faithful over a little; I will set you over much. Enter into the joy of your master." He also who had received the one talent came forward, saying, "Master, I knew you to be a hard man, reaping where you did not sow, and gathering where you scattered no seed, so I was afraid, and I went and hid your talent in the ground. Here you have what is yours." But his master answered him, "You wicked and slothful servant! You knew that I reap where I have not sown and gather where I scattered no seed? Then you ought to have invested my money with the bankers, and at my coming I should have received what was my own with interest. So take the talent from him and give it to him who has the ten talents… And cast the worthless servant into the outer darkness. In that place there will be weeping and gnashing of teeth.

- Matthew 25:14-28

This may be one of the most damning things ever said about God the Father. And Jesus, preparing to be crucified for the sake of God, absolutely had the right to say it. God gave the souls certain gifts at the divine separation – certain talents – will, consciousness, being. Then he just abandons the souls… with no word at all about what he wanted of them, or that he was expecting to reap where he had not sown. Then, when it suits him, he lobs back into town with: *"What have you got for me?"*

God did not give instructions to souls on how to increase what the souls started with because he himself was clueless that it would happen, that it could happen, that he wanted it to happen.

But there was one and only one way that God could reap this harvest: if souls were transformed by Baptism by Spirit and then, via the Holy Spirit, God could connect with them and learn through and from their journey.

Following in the footsteps of John the Baptist, Jesus had been singled out as a pivotal figure in this reaping of the souls. He was going to teach God what it was like to be a man. He was going to be a vehicle for God to learn what it was like to endure the ultimate in unjustified suffering.

Crucifixion.

Jesus died citing an Old Testament passage

Just before he died, Jesus screamed out arguably the most enigmatic words in human history: *"Eloi, Eloi, lema sabachthani? My God, my God, why have you forsaken me!?"*

So unexpected and confronting is this passage that it is sometimes referred to as "The Dereliction". The great apology for this Dereliction is that Jesus was quoting the beginning of Psalm 22 in the Old Testament which starts:

> My God, my God, why have you forsaken me?
> Why are you so far from saving me, from the
> words of my groaning?
> O my God, I cry by day, but you do not answer,
> and by night, but I find no rest.

The Psalm then goes on with a vivid portrayal of utter spiritual despair. It eventually turns the corner and ends up paying deference to God's power:

> All the ends of the earth shall remember
> and turn to the Lord,
> and all the families of the nations
> shall worship before you.
> For kingship belongs to the Lord,
> and he rules over the nations.

Sure, right, this is what Jesus was doing.

In body-racking agony, his lungs and heart collapsing, he summons up his last iota of strength to take one last deep breath so that he can scream out the beginning of a psalm with the clear-headed aim of getting bystanders to scurry to the local synagogue to look it up in the scrolls.

Hasn't this always been a popular practice for someone dying in breathless agony surrounded by illiterate people: they scream out a

book reference?
Seriously?

Part IV

The Enigma of the Cross

And Jesus uttered a loud cry and breathed his last. And the curtain of the temple was torn in two, from top to bottom.

- Mark 15:37-38

The Scream

When the nuclear explosion went off in Hiroshima, it vaporized people at Ground Zero. But people further out were not instantaneously vaporized. Instead, they were blasted by a tsunamic wave of radiation. If someone was standing between that wave and a wall, their silhouette – their image – would be seared into the wall by that flash of energy. Soon this person would die from radiation poisoning but their image would endure, branded into the wall.

As the body of Jesus was strangling itself on the Cross, the energy of God was as focused and concentrated as it could possibly be within the transformed, baptized-by-Spirit soul of Jesus.

God felt as Jesus felt... suffered as Jesus suffered... The scourging, the crown of thorns, the nails driven through the flesh, the humiliation, the sense of abandonment... God felt it all.

And Jesus endured it all in stony silence.

Death, mercifully, starts to slowly wind its way through Jesus's body.

There is a long-standing human belief that, on the point of death, the truth outs.... the veil that kept truth concealed is torn. One's life flashes before one's eyes. Deathbed confessions are counted as sacrosanct. In dark times, people were tortured to the edge of death because it was believed that, at that point of mortal agony, a person enters an altered state where the truth can no longer be contained.

Jesus hovered at this point.

From within the screaming depths of his physical agony, something wells up from the very core of Jesus's being, something beyond physical agony, something beyond emotional pain, something beyond earthly despair, something that will shatter the silence of the Cross.

It is the plaintive cry of the lost souls, of souls abandoned by God.

It is the scream of the birth trauma of the souls, of souls cast out of God's presence.

It is the bottomless despair of the rejected souls.

"Eloi, Eloi, lema sabachthani!?"
My God! My God! Why hast thou forsaken me!?

Each of us carries this scream, this agony, this trauma, this loneliness, this torment at the very core of our soul. And this agony had been torn from the depths of Jesus just as he was about to die.

This primal agony of the souls exploded and seared its way through God.

And God wasn't ready for it.

Not this level of torment.

Not this shock.

Not this slap across the face about his own role in the torment of souls.

He could not encompass it.

He could not handle it.

He could not maintain his link with Jesus.

God exploded out of his connection with Jesus.

Right at the moment of Jesus's despair on the Cross.

Like a nuclear bomb going off.

Like that bomb going off in Hiroshima, the spiritual explosion imprinted Jesus's image/energy on the spiritual universe. It imprinted it on the Holy Spirit.

And so it was that the course and character of the spiritual universe was changed in an instant.

Underneath your soul is the energetic field of the spiritual universe – the Holy Spirit, the One, Brahman – and imprinted on that universal spiritual field is Jesus in his moment of despair on the cross.

Like an image burnt onto a wall by a nuclear explosion.

Part V

The Aftermath

Those who say that the Lord first died and then arose are confused. For first he arose and (then) he died.

- Gospel of Philip 22

The Jesus Imprint

Deep within you, deep within the most rabid atheist, there runs a spiritual vibration, the spiritual field: the Self, the One, the Holy Spirit, Brahman.

And burnt onto that is the image of Jesus on the Cross.

This was the Resurrection.

This was the Ascension.

And it happened before Jesus died.

I am going to refer to it as the Imprinting.

Again and again, across gulfs in time and place and culture and conviction, the image of Jesus emerges in people doing inner work.

When, in 1991, in the course of my inner path, the image of Jesus complete with a crown of thorns came out of me, at first I refused to accept it or share it with anyone. I faced it only extremely reluctantly.[29]

Weeks later, one of my teachers shared with me that she had been surprised when, on her inner path, she encountered visions of Jesus – she being a good Jewish girl and all.

Stanislav Grof has found it happening, again and again and again, over and over and over, in people doing "holotropic breathwork":

> At this point, many people have, for example, visions of crucifixion or experience an agonizing identification with Jesus Christ on the Cross.
>
> - Grof, *The Cosmic Game*, p. 22

These identifications are not just with Jesus but **with Jesus on the Cross in the agony of crucifixion**. Grof found this happening not just in Westerners but also in people whose background was Buddhist, Shinto or Hindu.

Carl Jung found the image of Jesus Christ appearing again and again in the inner journey of his patients - and surely also in his own inner journey. In his book *Aion*, Jung dances around the issue, trying to explain this phenomenologically – how the "image of Christ" is the

---

[29] If you wish to know more about my inner journey, go to renlexander.com and follow me on YouTube: youtube.com/@drrenlexander

ideal image for the Self in our cultural context.

It has nothing to do with current cultural context. It is a universal imprinting.

In the 9th Century, Muslim mystics, Sufis, were so confronted by the image of Jesus in their inner spiritual path that they changed the Islamic catch-cry of "There is no God but Allah and Mohammed is his Messenger" to "There is no God but Allah and Jesus is his Messenger."[30]

During this period, the Muslim mystic Mansur al-Hallaj was imprisoned for 11 years for shouting out "I am the Truth!" Apparently the verbal expression of this mystic experience is blasphemy in Islam. He was eventually sentenced to be hacked to death. He declared that he wanted to die "in the supreme confession of the Cross".

His was to be one of the most amazing executions in human history. Al-Hallaj smiled as he was being hacked to pieces. When they cut off his legs, he said: "I used to walk the earth with these legs, now there's only one step to heaven, cut that if you can."

In 1899, Rudolf Steiner, the German philosopher/architect/esotericist, found himself in a spiritual crisis. "At that time I had to save my spiritual perception by inner battles." (*Autobiography*, p. 264). Prior to this, the 38-year-old Steiner had almost no interest in Christianity but now:

> …the real content of Christianity was beginning germinally to unfold within me as an inner phenomenon. About the turn of the century the germ unfolded more and more… The evolution of my soul rested upon the fact that I stood before the Mystery of Golgotha in most inward, earnest joy of knowledge.
>
> - Rudolf Steiner, *Autobiography*, p. 265.

Steiner came to see the crucifixion of Jesus as the pivotal point in the spiritual history of the planet. He described it as:

- point zero[31]

---

[30] See Karen Armstrong, *A History of God*, p. 225.

[31] Rudolf Steiner, "The three spiritual preliminary stages of the Mystery of Golgotha", *Approaching the Mystery of Golgotha*

- the turning point in human evolution[32]
- the greatest event that ever happened to all of humanity[33]
- a unique event which has supreme value for the whole of mankind[34].

Steiner came to perceive that this unique event changed forever the nature of mystic union:

> The union of the soul with its highest powers is at the same time union with the historical Christ.
>
> - Rudolf Steiner, *Christianity as Mystic Fact*, Chapter XI: "The Nature of Christianity".

In the 14th Century, the great Christian mystic Meister Eckhart wrote about how the image of Jesus was imprinted and how you had to pass through this.

> Christ says: "No one comes to the Father except through me." (John 14:6). Christ is the eternal image. Now the soul should not remain in him but rather must pass through him as he himself says.
>
> - Meister Eckhart, *Selected Writings*, p.146.

The Gospel of Philip, from around the 3rd Century A.D., similarly indicates the need to go through the Christ to be united with the Holy Spirit:

> Through the Holy Spirit we are indeed begotten again, but we are begotten through Christ in the two [i.e., in the Holy Spirit]. We are anointed

---

[32] Rudolf Steiner, "The Michael impulse and the mystery of Golgotha Part Two" in *Approaching the Mystery of Golgotha*

[33] Rudolf Steiner, "Christ at the time of the mystery of Golgotha and Christ in the Twentieth Century", *Approaching the Mystery of Golgotha*.

[34] Rudolf Steiner, *Christianity as Mystic Fact*, Chapter XII: "Christianity and Heathen Wisdom'.

through the Spirit. When we were begotten, we were united. (80; WI)

There is the Son of Mankind and there is the Grandson of Mankind. The Lord [Jesus] is the Son of Mankind, and the Grandson of Mankind is he who is created thru the Son of Mankind. (128) [35]

In the 16th Century, St Teresa of Avila likewise records that the union of the soul with Spirit involves not just the Holy Spirit but the whole of the Trinity (i.e., the image of Jesus as Christ as well):

By some mysterious manifestation of the truth, the three Persons of the most Blessed Trinity reveal themselves.

- St Teresa of Avila, *The Interior Castle*, "The Seventh Mansions", 1:9

From St Gregory of Palamas, the 14th Century Eastern Orthodox theologian:

For the kingdom of heaven or, rather, the King of heaven – ineffable in His generosity – is within us.

- *The Philokalia*, Topics of Natural and Theological Science, Volume Four.

Within us.
Within all of us.
Within you.

The shockwave

The spiritual field (the "Holy Spirit") which underlies every soul – and so every person – changed in that instant on the Cross. We would expect to see some sort of psychic change across humanity as a whole.

---

[35] Elsewhere the *Gospel of Philip* 37 says: "'the Holy Spirit' is a double name". I believe what he is trying to indicate here is that Jesus-as-Christ and Spirit are fused: two have become one.

We shall soon see powerful evidence of this in the otherwise inexplicable spread of Christianity. We can also date this exact moment of the Imprinting as bringing about an upheaval in what constituted spirituality and religion.

Up to this point, religion was all about doing things. Pagan religion was all about doing stuff which courted the favor of the gods: sacrificing and building temples to them so as to stay on their good side. Judaism, for all its belief in the One God, was the same: it was all about sacrificing to God at the Temple and obeying the seemingly endless requirements of the Jewish Law. If they prayed, it was out loud. The divine wasn't felt or experienced on the inside; it was seen in burning bushes and whirlwinds and dwelt within the Holy of Holies inside the deepest recesses of the Temple.

Nowadays, we simply take it for granted that religion is an *inner* thing. It is about inner faith, inner prayer, inner voices. This did not exist prior to that moment on the Cross. Christianity is all about faith in Jesus. Islam is all about faith in Allah.

This is the ripple effect from the shockwave that went out from that moment on the Cross. Something new was born within people. Spiritual eyes turned from the external to the internal.

> At the moment when the Mystery of Golgotha intervened, this great transition occurred from the life in the external surroundings to a turning inward.
>
> - Rudolf Steiner, "The Michael impulse and the mystery of Golgotha Part Two", Lecture Four in *Approaching the Mystery of Golgotha*

In the words of the Apostle Paul:

> And because you are sons, God has sent the Spirit of his Son into our hearts, crying, "Abba! Father!" (Galatians 4:6)

> Or do you not realize this about yourselves, that Jesus Christ is in you? (2 Corinthians 13:5)

I have been crucified with Christ. It is no longer I who live, but Christ who lives in me. (Galatians 2:20)

The parting of ways

The progress of science has been hindered by the belief, at any given time, that we knew nearly all of it and that any new phenomenon can obviously be explained in terms of what we already know.

- Eric Laithwaite, Gaze in Wonder, BBC Horizon documentary, 1989

Doubtless, by now, I have lost some readers – perhaps many readers.

Brains will be screaming out: *No, there must be some ordinary explanation for all this. Some ordinary, everyday explanation about how a hick preacher in a third-rate country in the Roman Empire became, far and away, the most famous and impactful person in human history. There must be an ordinary explanation for how people have unbidden visions of Jesus on their inner journey. There must be an ordinary explanation for it all. There must be. There has to be. There must be.*

There isn't.

There are two events so extraordinary that they do not admit of normal explanations. One of these is in prehistory. One of these is in recorded history.

The extraordinary one in recorded history is the mystery of the impact of Jesus – his impact on history and his impact on the consciousnesses of individuals. An impact which has seemingly not dimmed across time such that 2.5 billion people – a third of the human race – now profess faith in him.

The ordinary has ordinary explanations.

The rare may have ordinary explanations.

But the truly one-off and unique is not so likely to have an ordinary explanation. (Consider the birth of the physical universe.)

The Mystery of Golgotha… was a unique event in the evolution of the Earth, one that had never happened before in the same way and will never happen again in the same manner. Human understanding is always looking for a standard, for a comparison in relation to which things can be understood but something that is incomparable cannot be compared. Because it is unique, it is understood only with difficulty.

- Rudolf Steiner, *Approaching the Mystery of Golgotha*, Lecture Two: "Christ at the time of the mystery of Golgotha and Christ in the Twentieth Century"

Oh... but it's just because people are silly.

That is not an explanation. That is just a lame attempt to explain it away. Even accepting that people are "silly", we are still left with this question: *Why are they "silly" in this particular direction? Why are sane, articulate people consistently "silly" in this particular direction century after century, millennium after millennium?*

You know what would be really silly?

To believe that there can be effects without causes.

These unbidden – even resisted – mystic/psychological experiences associated with Jesus on the Cross exist. They must have a cause. Only the Imprinting can explain them. Only the Imprinting of Jesus onto the Holy-Spirit/Brahman/The-One can explain the otherwise inexplicable. The Imprinting explains many of the Jesus Delusions and much more besides:

- the symbol of the Cross
- belief in the resurrection
- the belief in the Second Coming
- the rewriting of Jesus's life
- the apostolic movement
- conversions
- the otherwise inexplicable spread of Christianity.

The symbol of the Cross

What is the pivotal symbol of Christianity?

It is the Cross.

If the greatest moment in Christianity was the physical resurrection of Jesus's body then why isn't that the dominant symbol of Christianity?

But, no, it's the Cross and Jesus on the Cross.

Why this strange anomaly?

Because, deep within each of us, on the Holy Spirit within our soul, there is imprinted that moment on the Cross.

And he rose again on the third day

How did a religion spread when it was based on the incredibly unlikely scenario that its pivotal figure was killed as a common criminal and then rose from the dead on the third day?

The answer lies in the Imprinting.

Deep within people, underneath the soul, on the Holy Spirit, has been imprinted the energy and image of Jesus. It is easy to believe in the resurrection of Jesus because Jesus was "resurrected" into eternity – even before he died. The Ascension had already taken place. Jesus still was "alive" because his image was there imprinted on the eternal Spirit.

The dawn of a new era

The Imprinting marked a new era in the spiritual universe.

As above, so below.

History was divided into before and after Jesus: B.C. and A.D.

But this dividing point should never have been at the point of his physical birth but his "birth" onto the Holy Spirit – the moment in time just before his death. That is the dividing point: the point that divides the B.C. from the A.D. of the spiritual universe.

The rewriting of Jesus's life

In the instant of the Imprinting, Jesus became more than man. He became eternalized.

He – or rather his Imprint – was born as a spiritual reality back then, still is now and perhaps will be for the rest of eternity. And the awareness of that, however distant and buried, lies inside each of us.

It lay inside the people writing the Gospels. They had a sense of the sanctification of Jesus, of his immortality, of his special place in the spiritual universe. As they did not know enough to date it from that instant just before his death, they ascribed this "sanctification" onto the whole of Jesus's life. The towering spiritual figure that Jesus became on the point of his death is backdated to even before he was born:

- He was the only begotten Son of God.
- He was born of a virgin.
- John the Baptist foretold of the coming of a man who would be so much greater than him.
- Jesus foretold that he would rise again after three days.
- Jesus was the Messiah, the anointed, the chosen one, the Son of God.

It's all mythologizing. It is all a backward projection of the pervasive spiritual figure that Jesus would become at the point just before his death.

Yeshua was born an ordinary man. He became special because of his inner work which led to the baptism of his soul. He became extraordinarily special because he was singled out by God to suffer for God so God could learn the lot of Man. And he became the most unique man in the spiritual history of our world through the Imprinting.

Surely this is a hugely more inspiring story than Jesus was already born the Son of God and that it was all foretold and pre-destined. Compared to the actual drama of Yeshua, that is just boring.

The Virgin birth of the Son of God

There are many bizarre things in faith-based Christianity but they don't get any more bizarre than the cult of the Virgin birth – the idea that Jesus was born a son of the Holy Spirit and a virgin woman.

Seriously?

That's about as ludicrous an idea as you can get. And yet, with the Imprinting, you can see why it gets some traction. Baptism of the soul happens when a purified soul ("Virgin'") becomes fused to the Holy Spirit. This gives rise to a "Son of Man" (of which Jesus was one example). Jesus was not "the only begotten Son of God". But, in a sense, his Imprint was. When God exploded out of Jesus, it imprinted Jesus's image/energy onto the Holy Spirit. This Imprint could be said to be the "Son of God". In the words of the Gospel of Philip, Jesus was "begotten in the Spirit by God".

> "My God, my God, why oh Lord [did] thou abandon me?" – he spoke these (words) on the cross. For he divided the place... having been begotten in the Spirit by God.
>
> - Gospel of Philip 77

Disciples become Apostles

One of the bizarrest twists in the whole saga...

When Jesus was arrested, his disciples could not run away fast enough. The only people to turn up to his crucifixion were a few of his female followers. After his crucifixion, these very same quaking male disciples are abruptly transformed into fearless apostles. Whatever threats are made against them, they keep spreading the word about Jesus. Threats of imprisonment, they are unfazed. Threats of death – bring it on.

The word "martyr" originally came from Greek and it meant "witness" or "bear witness". The word evolved to mean sacrificing one's life for faith in Jesus the Christ. No longer did these men run for their lives. Instead, they were literally happy to be killed for bearing witness. It was considered a privilege and a rite of passage to be martyred.

112

How bizarre is that?

That bespeaks of an absolute inner transformation. But what these apostles bore witness to was not the same message that Jesus preached. Jesus was martyred for preaching the kingdom of God. This is not what the apostles were dying for. Instead, the apostles emphasized the Holy Spirit and the difference that Jesus has made *inside them*.

To see how the apostles' focus radically and suddenly shifted, we only need to consider the Gospel of Luke and the Acts of the Apostles. These two books were written by the same author. Taken together, they form a sprawling narrative that constitutes about a quarter of the New Testament.

In the Gospel of Luke, the kingdom of God is mentioned 32 times and the Holy Spirit 13 times. When the author moves on to describing the acts of the apostles, the balance radically changes: the kingdom of God is only mentioned a paltry six times and the Holy Spirit is mentioned a staggering 42 times. That is a monumental upheaval in emphasis.

This trend is also throughout the letters of Paul.

This titanic shift all makes sense in terms of the Imprinting. The Imprinting changed the appearance of the Holy Spirit inside each of us. No longer is it a neutral energy. It has been personalized by the Imprinting of Jesus on it. In a sense, Jesus now dwelt within each of the apostles. Certainly that is what the early apostles fearlessly preached.

Only the Imprinting can make sense of such a radical shift.

The spread of Christianity

Yet, against all odds, by the third century, Christianity had become a force to be reckoned with. We still do not really understand how this came about.

- Karen Armstrong, *Fields of Blood: Religion and the History of Violence*, p. 172.

The spread of Christianity is one of the great mysteries of recorded human history. If you look at the dissemination of major religions, there is none that is as hard to explain as the spread of Christianity.

The Buddha preached and taught for 45 years. His words were repeated and immortalized into beautiful Pali chants. Yet nowadays, in its birthplace of India, Buddhism is only the 5th most popular religion behind Hindu, Islam, Sikh and Christianity.

For 23 years, Mohammed channeled writings from a discarnate entity claiming to be the Archangel Gabriel (Jibril). This became the Qur'an. Based on this, Mohammed set out to start a new religion, claiming he was the greatest prophet of all time. His religion spread, in part, because the text is apparently stunningly beautiful in its original Arabic. Arguably far more important were military conquests. Mohammed moved from being a pacifist preacher into being a warlord.

If the Gospel of Mark is to be the guide, Jesus may have taught for about a year. From the time of John the Baptist's arrest (and so the start of Jesus preaching) to Jesus's crucifixion on the cross... perhaps a year. If we take the timeline of the Gospel of John, it only blows the period out to around three years.

How massive has been the impact of these couple of years on the history of the planet?

And Jesus was not even the originator of this new teaching. John the Baptist was. Try to get your head around this in terms of Buddhism or Islam. It would be as if the key person being revered was not Buddha or Mohammed but a student who was just passing the teaching on.

Moreover, neither John nor Jesus was even trying to start a new religion. They both considered themselves to be good Jewish boys. They wrote nothing down. In the early days, the Jesus movement was spread by word of mouth. It took centuries for the Church to settle on the official New Testament. Even then, it was largely preserved in Latin. Later, the Church fought tooth and nail to stop it being translated into common languages. People were burnt at the stake for translating the Bible into local languages which people could actually comprehend.

And the official Gospels are a mess. There are contradictions between them. There is a chasm of difference between the three synoptic Gospels and the Gospel of John.

Forget about spreading the word by military conquest. It could not have been more the polar opposite in the early centuries: Christians were ostracized, they had their property confiscated, they were imprisoned, tortured and killed.

How the hell did Christianity spread? How did so many people come to accept a religion in which the instigator died ignominiously on the Cross as a criminal? How did people come to accept the seemingly preposterous idea that, on the third day, he rose again from the dead?

The apostles spreading the word did not focus on his life and teachings but on his ignominious death and alleged resurrection. And their big argument for this was not the physical reanimation of Jesus's corpse but instead the changes that the reborn Jesus had wrought inside each of them.

Let's summarize the story...

There was an obscure Jewish preacher, a student of John the Baptist, from an embarrassingly insignificant village, Nazareth, wandering around the countryside of a backwater country in the Roman Empire. For maybe a couple of years, he preaches to illiterate peasants in parables which virtually none of them understand. He doesn't ever write anything down to preserve his thoughts. He is arrested and virtually all his disciples turn their backs on him and run away. Only hours later he is crucified as a common criminal.

That is the end of that obscure little drama, right? The life of Jesus will be discarded into the dustbin of history.

But instead Jesus would become the most famous man in human history. He would influence more of history than any other person.

Within 25 years of his ignominious execution, there are Christian communities – not just the odd conversion here or there – but communities in:

- Jerusalem and elsewhere in Palestine
- Syria
- Asia Minor (Turkey)
- Greece
- Italy (yes even in Rome)

And, of course, it just went on and on from there. In an era of no mass communications, little travel and near-universal illiteracy.

How could that happen?

The answer lies in the Imprinting. It left a trace of Jesus deep inside each of us.

Christ would never have made the impression he did on his followers if he had not expressed something that was alive and at work in their unconscious. Christianity would never have spread through the pagan world with such astonishing rapidity had its ideas not found an analogous psychic readiness to receive them.

- Carl Jung, *Answer to Job*, p.79.

Nowdays people have heads stuffed full of "facts". They are convinced they know things; that they are scientific. Western atheists now conflate the disbelief in a benign all-powerful all-good all-knowing God with a disbelief in all spirituality. They are convinced that tomorrow belongs to them. And yet the Imprint of Jesus remains. As people in the West contract themselves into games, Christianity is still the biggest religion in the world.

And it's spreading.

China is racing towards 100 million Christians. This from four million Christians in 1954.

It is estimated that by 2025, there will be over 760 million Christians in Africa. This from nine million in 1900.

Even now, apparently the most common delusion in psychiatric wards is that the person thinks he is Jesus Christ. In part, this is because some of these unfortunates sense the imprint of Jesus deep within them and lack the proper boundaries to put this instinct into perspective.

Even now, in the West, where people are trained to be more interested in games than spiritual matters, there abides an ineluctable fascination with Jesus. Mega-hits such as *The Da Vinci Code, The Passion of the Christ, The Bible* TV series and *Killing Jesus* bear eloquent testimony that there remains a profound inner fascination with a construction worker from Nazareth. Such things happen because, deep with each of us, there is a sliver of the One/Brahman/the Holy-Spirit, and on that sliver is imprinted the image and energy of Jesus.

Modern faith-based Christianity is an abomination. It does not reflect one thing that John the Baptist and Jesus were actually on about. There is so much chasing your own spiritual tail – praying and singing and praising the Lord – but no actual spiritual inner growth. No Baptism by the Holy Spirit.

116

But this is not the fault of the followers. They sense a reality. They sense that there is some connection with Jesus inside them. It is arguably the responsibility of the leaders – those people who have assumed leadership positions and recited the words of the Bible while understanding nothing of Baptism by the Holy Spirit and the kingdom of God. This was Jesus's major annoyance with the Pharisees – that they were misguidedly standing in the way of the genuine spiritual evolution of themselves and others.

> But woe to you, scribes and Pharisees, hypocrites!
> For you shut the kingdom of heaven in people's
> faces. For you neither enter yourselves nor allow
> those who would enter to go in.
>
> - Matthew 23:13

Absolutely exactly the same accusation could be leveled at present-day religious leaders. Now they are the Pharisees.

Christianity should never have been about faith. It needs to be about the purification of your soul so that it can merge with the Universal Spirit, so that you can become involved in the only game that really matters: your soul's healing and evolution, and the evolution of the spiritual universe.

As Jesus was.

As you can be.

This is what Christianity is supposed to be about: getting to Baptism by the Holy Spirit. In the words of the Gospel of Philip:

> If one goes down into the water and comes up
> without having received anything, and says "I am a
> Christian," he has borrowed the name at interest.
> But if he receives the Holy Spirit, he has the name
> as a gift. He who has received a gift does not have
> to give it back… (63; WI)

I honestly wish that having faith in Jesus, praying to him and calling out his name ecstatically in Church will evolve your soul. It won't. Only deep inner work can enable you to tread the path that Jesus trod.

Whatever became of God?

The Old Testament portrays a God that was interested in humankind – in particular, the Israelite people. He was prepared to stick his nose in and communicate with Moses and Job and Elijah. Parts of the Old Testament really look like God was experimenting with the Israelite tribe.

But there has not been any evidence of such activity since the Imprinting. Since the crucifixion of Jesus, we can find examples of mystics who have had their souls baptized-by-Spirit: Meister Eckhart, Plotinus, St Teresa of Avila, St John of the Cross, St Gregory of Palamas and who knows how many silent mystics. What we can't see is any evidence that such transformed souls (which have thereby been entered into the "kingdom of God") have, in any way, been contacted by God the Father. We can't see any passages from mystics that sound like the Transfiguration.

God has not been active in the kingdom of God.

So what happened to God??

That is unknowable but I believe that there are only two possibilities:

1. God is in shock

In shock for the last two thousand years? Sure... what's two thousand years more or less to God? The wrenching epiphany of *Eloi, Eloi, lema sabachthani!? My God! My God! Why hast thou forsaken me!?* was too much for him. It put him into shock. Perhaps every time in last two thousand years that a soul experiences baptism-by-Spirit, this chips away at the healing of the spiritual universe – and God is given some salve to come out of his shock. Or... another possibility...

2. God was reabsorbed back into the Holy Spirit

As discussed in Part III of this book, that which is called "God" was originally condensed out of the Holy Spirit in order to spawn souls. What was left over after this spawning of the souls was "God the Father". Perhaps the Imprinting was God the Father being reabsorbed back into the Holy Spirit. This would not be a spiritual tragedy. Recall that Jesus rated the Holy Spirit above "God":

"Truly, I say to you, all sins will be forgiven the children of man, and whatever blasphemies they utter, but whoever blasphemes against the Holy Spirit never has forgiveness, but is guilty of an eternal sin."

- Mark 3:28-29

The Apocalypse that never was

One of the fallouts of the Imprinting was that the apocalyptic reckoning of souls foreshadowed by Jesus never happened. Jesus believed that the Son of Man (the soul of John the Baptist) would come in clouds of glory and that there would be a reckoning of souls – the evil and hopeless ones would be wiped out. But things did not go the way of the Apocalypse... the cosmic drama takes a dramatic sideways turn… the despair of Jesus on the cross.... the shock to God... the Imprinting.

The New Covenant was broken.

If there was to be a God-driven apocalypse – an intervention by God and the Son of Man to rectify the injustices of the world – it got canned at that moment. God went into shock and whatever might have happened did not happen. If Jesus did believe that an Intervention from God was coming, he himself changed all that in that final instant on the Cross.

It was the Apocalypse that never was.

True believers in rapture

But belief in a forthcoming reckoning of souls did not die. Instead this idea became more public and was heavily proselytized by the Apostolic Fathers of the Christian Movement – by the Apostle Paul in particular. But the performing cast of The Apocalypse was radically overhauled. The Son of Man was thrown out the window. Instead, it was transmogrified into the Second Coming of Jesus the Christ, Jesus the Lord, Jesus the Savior:

For the Lord himself [i.e., Jesus] will descend from heaven with a cry of command, with the voice of

> an archangel, and with the sound of the trumpet of
> God. And the dead in Christ will rise first. Then
> we who are alive, who are left, will be caught up
> together with them in the clouds to meet the Lord
> in the air, and so we will always be with the Lord.
>
> - 1 Thessalonians 4:16-17

We can see why the Imprinting might lead to a belief in a Second Coming of Jesus. The Imprinting of Jesus's image onto the Holy Spirit meant that there already had been a second coming of Jesus: his image had been imprinted on the "soul within a soul" of each of us. Jesus has already made a Second Coming. It makes it pretty easy to believe in a Second Coming when you have his Imprint deep within you. But the actual Second Coming never did actually come. Paul expected to witness it before he died. Paul died with no apocalypse. All the apostles died. No apocalypse. No reckoning of souls. No Second Coming.

But the belief in the apocalyptic Second Coming of Jesus did not die. It remained and it shaped European history in fundamental ways. Thomas Cromwell and Martin Luther both came to believe that the apocalypse was imminent and their belief shaped a lot of their actions. Arguably, these two laid the ground for the secular democracy which now dominates most of the globe.

More recent Christian apocalyptic believers have favored the term "the Rapture" rather than "Second Coming". This is a term derived from Latin and means "a carrying off". The theory, derived from the epistles of Paul, is that The Big Spiritual Bang will start with the Rapture: Christ will appear in the sky and gather up the true believers – gathering them up into the air. Following this, there will be a period of Great Tribulation for the rest of humanity.

The failed predictions of apocalyptic soothsayers have not put off the next generation of soothsayers. Some recent examples...

In the first half of the 19th Century, William Miller preached that the second coming of Christ was going to happen around 1844. This was based on his careful analysis of the Bible. Believers became known as "Millerites". There were thousands of them. Pressed to give a more accurate time, Miller settled on between March 21, 1843 and March 21, 1844. These twelve months came and went. A hurried recalculation. April 18th, 1844. This day also came and went...

Enter Samuel S. Snow who, in a blaze of Biblical mathematics, announced that the exact date was October 22nd, 1844. Midnight on that day tolled with no appearance from Jesus. It became known as The Great Disappointment. It was especially disappointing for those Millerites who had given away all their possessions in anticipation. Ouch. Some went to court trying to get their property back.

In 1970, Hal Lindsey, an American evangelist, published *The Late, Great Planet Earth* which, based on careful analysis of Biblical passages, predicted that the Rapture was just around the corner, at one stage citing 1988. His book sold 28 million copies. In 1979, a U.S. film based on it became the biggest domestically-made film of the year.

Getting closer to 1988, Edgar C. Whisenant, a former NASA engineer, published a book called *88 Reasons Why the Rapture Will Be in 1988*. Specifically, it would be between September 11th and 13th, 1988. Three hundred thousand copies were mailed free of charge to ministers across America. 4.5 million copies were sold.

When September 14th rolled around uneventfully, Whisenant pinpointed a technicality to do with the advent of calendars and dated it in 1989.

When 1990 rolled around, he made another adjustment.

You get the idea.

An alternative reality

The Imprinting from Jesus' despair on the Cross was a turning point in the spiritual universe. It blindsided God. It pushed the course of the spiritual universe in a different direction. Which leaves us with a fascinating question: *What might have been?*

If God's education had only been limited to a human level of suffering and he had not been overwhelmed by the despair of the souls, what might have been?

Having experienced human suffering, God the Father might have become capable of understanding things he was never capable of before. He might have understood morality and injustice. He might have become capable of compassion. Would he have then compassionately and ruthlessly intervened to wipe out the wicked? Could he have? Was he capable of doing that?

Who knows?

Perhaps God may not have been capable of a physical intervention but perhaps he may have been capable of a spiritual intervention – of destroying souls, of destroying the worst of souls.

Who knows?

Was that moment of Jesus's utter soul-level despair on the Cross a good thing or a bad thing? Would the world be a better place if it hadn't happened?

Who knows?

No-one.

Part VI

Preaching the Kingdom of Jesus

"I must preach the good news of the kingdom of God..."

- Jesus, Luke 4:43.

For this very reason, make every effort to supplement your faith with virtue... For in this way there will be richly provided for you an entrance into the eternal kingdom of our Lord and Savior Jesus Christ.

- 2 Peter 1:5, 11

Exit the historical Jesus

Our story of the life and teachings of Jesus has come to an end. But there remains an unresolved portion of a greater jigsaw puzzle: *Whatever happened to the teachings of John the Baptist and Jesus?*

How did the teachings of these two great Jewish mystics about the inner evolution of the soul become a brand new religion that was all about faith in Jesus as Savior?

John the Baptist and Jesus were the great democratizers of spirituality. Whoever you were – prostitute or prophet, prince or pauper, pariah or priest – you had exactly the same chance to transform your soul and realize the kingdom of God. Indeed, there were advantages in being a prostitute, pauper or pariah: you would have more motivation to embrace the inner path.

How did it get from that to Jesus being worshipped as the Son of God? How did Jesus's teachings about the inner kingdom of God get thrown out the window?

The Din of Chaos

In the days and weeks and months following Jesus's death, chaos reigned…

- **Fear!** Disciples in terror of their lives.

- **Grief!** Devastating grief at the loss of their beloved teacher.

- **Guilt!** At not being there for Jesus and running away.

- **Anger!** At Judas, the high priests, the Romans.

- **Wonder!** What was going on inside them? When they thought about Jesus, there was a dawning awareness of something new inside.

- **Confusion!** Rumors of sightings of Jesus.

- **Disputes!** Even the people who saw an image of someone couldn't agree about whether it was Jesus or not.

- **Conversions of unbelievers!** Sightings of Jesus were beginning to convert people to Jesus in a new way. One sighting of Jesus turned James, one of the brothers of Jesus who had rejected him, into a devout believer. These new converts had never studied under Jesus but they would come to lay claim to positions of authority within the Jesus movement.

- **Wild speculations!** As more sightings of Jesus came through there was increasing speculation about what happened to his body. Could he have come back from the dead? Was there something even more special about Jesus than he had let slip during his lifetime?

- **The end is coming!!!** All this chaos, these sightings of the dead, this cascade of emotions... surely this confirmed that this was an end of times... an apocalypse was coming...

- **Desperate search for clarity!** As people are wont to do in times of distress, they turned to the Bible for answers – or, to be less anachronistic, they turned to Jewish scripture. The distressed followers latched onto any scriptural passages which somehow seemed relevant and/or might help explain the life, suffering and death of Jesus. We shall see that passages in the Book of Isaiah came to be interpreted as predicting the coming of a suffering Messiah. Such passages would come to shape the oral tradition about Jesus and then the four Gospels. If you think that Jesus was the fulfillment of predictions in the Old Testament, it is because the Gospels were written to make his life look that way. For example, the Gospel of Luke has the ridiculous scenario of a universal census which forces people to return to the place of their birth (Luke 2:1-7). This is put in to explain how Jesus was really born in Bethlehem because "the Messiah" had to come out of the City of David and could not possibly have come from an embarrassing hick town like Nazareth. (See Micah 5:2 and Matt 2:5-6)

Out of this din of thoughts and overpowering emotions, ideas would emerge that could have never been foreseen before the crucifixion... ideas that would give birth to a new religion... ideas that would powerfully shape the history of our planet.

Added confusion: the words of the Son of Man

We have seen that Jesus used the term "the Son of Man" in two ways: to refer to himself and to refer to an apocalyptic Son of Man (the spirit of John the Baptist) who was going to appear after Jesus's death and lead a reckoning of souls. After the crucifixion, this dual usage would lead to two great confusions.

First great confusion: The Second Coming

Soon after the crucifixion, there were sightings of Jesus. As such, it became very easy to make the leap that it would be Jesus (that Son of Man) who would lead the reckoning of souls – and not another, third-party Son of Man (John the Baptist). And so it was that, perhaps quite rapidly, the predicted reckoning of souls led by the Son of Man transmuted into the Second Coming of Jesus: Jesus was going to appear in the sky and judge all souls. (More on this soon.)

Second great confusion: Jesus predicted his return from the dead

> "…you will see the Son of Man seated at the right hand of Power, and coming with the clouds of heaven."
>
> - Mark 14:62

Over time, Jesus's prediction that the Son of Man was going to appear from heaven devolved into a prediction by Jesus that he himself was going to come back from the dead. Consider this statement by Jesus just after the Transfiguration:

> And as they were coming down the mountain, he charged them to tell no one what they had seen, until the Son of Man had risen from the dead.
>
> - Mark 9:9

Here Jesus is talking about the return of the original Son of Man (John the Baptist) but it could be misinterpreted as Jesus predicting his own return from the dead. Indeed, his statement confuses the disciples:

> So they kept the matter to themselves, questioning
> what this rising from the dead might mean.
>
> - Mark 9:10

The sightings of Jesus after his death cast a very new light on anything Jesus said about the coming of an apocalyptic Son of Man. Suddenly his words seemed much more like a prediction of his own return from the dead.

The Gospel of Mark has Jesus make three predictions about coming back from the dead:

> "Then he began to teach them that the Son of Man must undergo great suffering, and be rejected by the elders, the chief priests, and the scribes, and be killed, and after three days rise again." (Mark 8:31)

> "The Son of Man is to be betrayed into human hands, and they will kill him and three days after being killed, he will rise again." (Mark 9:31).

> "See, we are going up to Jerusalem, and the Son of Man will be delivered over to the chief priests and the scribes, and they will condemn him to death and deliver him over to the Gentiles. And they will mock him and spit on him, and flog him and kill him. And after three days he will rise." (Mark 10:33-34)

Note that all three of these predictions reference "the Son of Man" and all three are delivered in the third person as if Jesus was talking about someone else. This adds significant weight to the theory that Jesus was originally talking about the return of the apocalyptic Son of Man (i.e., John the Baptist) and, over time, this was transmuted and imaginatively re-cast into Jesus predicting his own return.

The idea that the historical Jesus predicted his resurrection to his disciples is extremely dubious because, if he had, his disciples would not have run away in terror when he was arrested and certainly they would not have been so disbelieving of reports that Jesus's body had risen (Luke 24:11) and been seen by others (John 20:24-29).

Added confusion: the actions of the Son of Man

Not only the words but the actions of Jesus created fog in the minds of the disciples. We have seen that, in an effort to get himself crucified, Jesus imitated Messiah-like actions. He entered Jerusalem on a donkey like a kingly Messiah. He trashed the Temple like a militant Messiah.

Despite the fact that, in the entire Gospel of Mark, Jesus never says he is the Messiah, such Messiah-like actions, abetted by post-crucifixion sightings of Jesus, led at least one key disciple to a rock-solid conviction that Jesus was the Messiah. This key disciple was Peter who had already leapt to this mistaken idea even before Jesus headed to Jerusalem (Mark 8:27-29).

In order to sell themselves the idea that Jesus was the Messiah, believers had to come up with a completely new concept of what a "Messiah" was. The Messiah was supposed to be a triumphal, liberating figure for the whole of Israel – and certainly not crucified in ignominy.

It was particularly hard for Jews to swallow the idea that Jesus was the Messiah foretold in ancient Jewish scripture because Deuteronomy 21:23 specifically said that anyone who is hung upon a tree (as happens in crucifixion) is cursed. How could the triumphal Messiah be cursed?

To get around this, Jesus-believers turned to other parts of Jewish scripture. The Old Testament is huge so chances were good that they would find something that seemed relevant to Jesus. They found it in the Book of Isaiah.[36] In particular, Chapter 53 was reinterpreted as a prediction that there would be a future suffering Messiah who would take on the sins of the world – despite the fact that the entire Book of Isaiah never mentions the "Messiah". As we shall see, the Book of Isaiah came to shape the four Gospels.

---

[36] To be discussed in some detail when examining the idea that Jesus took upon the sins of the world.

Beyond being given the mantle of "Messiah", Jesus was soon to be crowned the Son of God.

The Son of Man becomes the Son of God

Jesus occasionally describes himself as "Son of Man". He never referred to himself as "the Son of God" – certainly not in the most historically reliable gospel, the Gospel of Mark. Even in the other two synoptic Gospels (Matthew and Luke), there is nowhere that the words "I am the Son of God" come out of Jesus's mouth.

So why did followers come to believe that Jesus was "the Son of God"?

There were at least three key reasons:

1. Jesus had told his disciples that, upon his baptism by the Holy Spirit, he had heard the words "You are my Son". (Variations on this in Mark, Matthew and Luke) The conclusion should be that this makes him a Son of the Holy Spirit but it came to be regarded as the voice of God referring to Jesus as his one and only Son.

2. Oral tales of Jesus started to be told in Greek. Most Greek-speakers expected special people not to be a "Son of Man" but the offspring of a god – like Hercules, Pericles, the Roman Emperors, etc.

3. Sightings of Jesus seemed like proof that he came back from the dead which seems pretty Son-of-God-like.

The deceased Son of Man's ascension to "Son of God" was not instantaneous. It was a gradual process of increasingly more grandiose divination.

The letters of the Apostle Paul were written between 50 and 58 AD. Paul believed that Jesus was born flesh but became the Son of God at his resurrection – or at least this is the miracle which proved he was the Son of God.

> ...his Son, who was descended from David according to the flesh and was declared to be the Son of God in power according to the Spirit of

holiness by his resurrection from the dead, Jesus
Christ our Lord…

- Romans 1:3-4

The first Biblical Gospel written down was the Gospel of Mark. It starts with John the Baptist and the baptism of Jesus by the Holy Spirit. This seems to be the point at which Mark thinks Jesus became the Son of God.

The next two written Gospels, the Gospels of Matthew and Luke, have Jesus become the Son of God right at back at his conception: when Mary is inseminated by the Holy Spirit. (Of course, amazingly, even under these stories, Jesus should have been known as "a Son of the Holy Spirit" rather than "the Son of God".)

The last of the canonical Gospels, the Gospel of John, starts with "In the beginning was the Word." This Gospel has Jesus as the Son of God since the beginning of all creation – and he lowered himself by assuming earthly form. The humble carpenter-turned-mystic who described himself as "Son of Man" was no more. Behold the only begotten Son of God.

The kingdom of God becomes the Kingdom of Jesus

It was not just Jesus's sober self-assessment ("Son of Man") and his humility which were thrown out the window; so too were his teachings about the kingdom of God.

Arguably the Apostle Paul considered Jesus's actual teachings as largely irrelevant because any day now the resurrected Jesus was going to appear in the sky and gather up the faithful and desolate the unfaithful. So what Jesus said was not important; what was important was to have faith in Jesus and his resurrection.

One way to trace the prominence of an idea is track the number of times the term is used. The phrase "kingdom of God" is used 67 times in the New Testament. The Gospel of Matthew uses the equivalent phrase of "kingdom of heaven" 31 times. This gives us a total of 98 usages across the two terms. Here is the breakdown[37]:

Mark	14	(Mark is far shorter than the other Gospels)
		(includes 31 uses of the phrase
Matthew	36	"kingdom of heaven")
Luke	32	
John	2	
Acts of the Apostles	6	
Pauline Epistles[38]	6	

In the remainder of the New Testament, the phrase "kingdom of God" is used twice.

The last-penned of the Gospels was the Gospel of John. This Gospel admits that it was "written so that you may believe that Jesus is the Christ, the Son of God and that by believing you may have life in his name" (John 20:31). In line with that focus, teachings of the kingdom of God are thrown out the window with a paltry two mentions in the entire Gospel(and both those two mentions are in one brief – but revealing – conversation).[39]

Paul scarcely uses the phrase "the kingdom of God" but when he does, he obviously does not have the slightest clue that it was a phrase used by John the Baptist and Jesus to refer to something on the inner spiritual path. He uses it to refer to where the good and faithful will go after judgment by Jesus:

---

[37] Counts of word usage done using biblestudytools.com on the English Standard Version.

[38] I am taking the Pauline Epistles to be just those seven epistles that virtually all scholars agree are definitely by Paul: First Thessalonians, Philippians, Philemon, First Corinthians, Galatians, Second Corinthians, and Romans. See discussion in Appendices·

[39] John 3:4-5. Indeed the fact that this conversation makes it into the Gospel of John despite the author's obvious indifference to "the kingdom of God" actually adds historical credibility to it. It makes the cut even though it is dissimilar to the interests of the author.

> Or do you not know that the unrighteous will not inherit the kingdom of God? Do not be deceived: neither the sexually immoral, nor idolaters, nor adulterers, nor men who practice homosexuality, nor thieves, nor the greedy, nor drunkards, nor revilers, nor swindlers will inherit the kingdom of God. And such were some of you. But you were washed, you were sanctified, you were justified in the name of the Lord Jesus Christ and by the Spirit of our God.
>
> - 1 Corinthians 6:9-11.

The historical Jesus never founded a new religion. He was a Jewish preacher teaching about the inner spiritual path – the potential every Israelite had to transform their soul and enter into the kingdom of God. But the faith-based Christianity that developed after his death did not preach the kingdom of God. It preached the kingdom of Jesus.

> He [God] has delivered us from the domain of darkness and transferred us to the kingdom of his beloved Son, in whom we have redemption, the forgiveness of sins.
>
> - Colossians 1:13-14

The Apostolic Age

The early spreading of embryonic Christianity is called the Apostolic Age: it starts with the commissioning of the Twelve (commonly called "the Apostles') by Jesus around 29 AD and ends at around 100 AD when it is suggested that the last of the Twelve died – supposedly John. Of course, not all the emissaries of this period were one of the Twelve.

Records are scant but we can have confidence in the existence and influence of three pivotal figures in the early Jesus movement:

1. **The Disciple Peter** who completely misinterpreted what Jesus is about, bizarrely believing him to be the "Messiah" (Mark 8:29). This is the disciple who so irritates Jesus that he scathingly rebukes him: "Get behind me, Satan!" (Mark 8:33)

– compare this to Judas whom he calls "Friend" (Matt 26:50). This is the disciple who is so flabbergasted by the Transfiguration that he bizarrely suggests putting up tents in its honor. "For he did not know what to say, for they were terrified." (Mark 9:6) (So much for the idea that Peter had special insight into the nature of Jesus.) This is the disciple who is the least steadfast one, denying Jesus three times after his arrest (Mark 14:66-72). One can't help but think that some of the ridiculous over-the-top beliefs inculcated in the early Christian movement – like Jesus was the "Son of God" and the Jewish Messiah – may have been a result of Peter's guilt-ridden over-compensation. The portrayal of Peter in non-Biblical early Christian literature is sometimes not at all flattering. In the Gospel of Thomas (114), Peter is misogynistic, asking Jesus to "Make Mary [Magdalene] leave us, for females don't deserve life". In the Gospel of Mary (10:3-10), Peter is also misogynistic – expressing disbelief that Jesus could have revealed things to a woman that he didn't reveal to male disciples. He reduces Mary Magdalene to tears and is described by another male disciple as "hot-headed". The more I look at the behavior of the disciple who was originally called "Simon", the more I am inclined to think that his nickname of Peter/Cephas (i.e., "Rock") was not a reference to his steadfastness but to his thick-headedness and stubbornness.

2. **The Apostle Paul** who never even met the living Jesus and shows an almost complete disinterest in anything Jesus might have actually said. Prior to his conversion, Paul was a Pharisee dedicated to brutally persecuting followers of Jesus. Again, as in the case of Peter, one has to wonder about guilt-ridden over-compensation.

3. **James the Just** who rose to be head of the Jerusalem chapter of the Jesus Movement because he was Jesus's brother. James was never a disciple of Jesus. Like the rest of his family, when he first heard about his brother starting to preach, he was freaked out by it (Mark 3:20-35). James was converted to the Jesus movement by a post-crucifixion sighting of Jesus (1 Corinthians 15:7). Again we see the possibility of guilt-ridden

over-compensation arising out of his rejection of his brother when he was living.

Not exactly your ideal group to carry on and preserve the actual teachings of Jesus.

Moreover, they could not even agree among themselves: there were vigorous and even bitter disagreements between them.[40]

Paul and Peter were active travelers and spreaders of the Jesus movement in the northeast of the Mediterranean – from Judea across to Italy. They were both martyred in Rome.

The headquarters of the early Jesus movement was universally acknowledged to be Jerusalem. Whatever records kept there were wiped from the face of the Earth in 70 AD when the Romans put the city to the sword as part of quashing the Jewish rebellion.

What did survive and thrive were the epistles of St Paul.

In considering the Apostolic Age, there is one key thing to keep in mind: *Victors write the histories.* The letters of Paul appear in the New Testament because his version of Christianity prevailed. A lot of Paul's writings to early Christian communities were taken up with trying to mitigate against the influence of other teachers and to bind the communities to his teachings.

The 1945 discovery of early Christian literature at Nag Hammadi[41] confirmed that there were other, very different Jesus-following communities out there in the early centuries. Some of these communities were very focused on an inner path of spiritual evolution. We don't know nearly enough about such communities but some of their literature is electrifying: the famous Gospel of Thomas which has been described as "the Fifth Gospel" and the equally electrifying Gospel of Philip written sometime between 150 AD and 350 AD. I only discovered this latter "Gospel" after I started working on this book. I was stunned at how in alignment some of its passages are with what I was writing. Many of the key points in this present book can be found in the Gospel of Philip: the union of the soul and Spirit (Gospel of Philip 64, 89, 108, 120, etc), the importance of the body as necessary for this (25), even the Imprinting (22, 77). One passage even

---

[40] There is a very good discussion of this in Chapters 14 and 15 of Reza Aslan, *Zealot.*

[41] See Appendix Two

specifically cites and contradicts Paul (25). In the Gospel of Philip, the whole point of being Christian is to experience baptism by the Holy Spirit:

> If one goes down into the water and comes up without having received anything, and says "I am a Christian," he has borrowed the name at interest. But if he receives the Holy Spirit, he has the name as a gift. He who has received a gift does not have to give it back... (63; WI)

In receiving this anointment (Baptism by the Holy Spirit), one is linked back to Jesus on the Cross and becomes a Christ (i.e., anointed):

> He who has been anointed possesses everything. He possesses the resurrection, the light, the cross, the Holy Spirit. (101, WI)

> But one receives the unction [anointment]... of the power of the cross... this person is no longer a Christian but a Christ. (72 WI)

> There is the Son of Mankind and there is the Grandson of Mankind. The Lord [Jesus] is the Son of Mankind, and the Grandson of Mankind is he who is created thru the Son of Mankind. (128)

> Through the Holy Spirit we are indeed begotten again, but we are begotten through Christ in the two. We are anointed through the Spirit. When we were begotten, we were united. (80 WI)

Once this union happens, it is eternal and can never be broken: "...those who have united in the bridal chamber will no longer be separated." (Gospel of Philip 86, WI)

The Gospel makes extensive use of an image frequently used by mystics throughout the ages for the union of soul and spirit: the joining of a man/bridegroom with a wife/bride/virgin. It specifically tags earthly conjoining as being an analogy for mystic union:

Mating occurs in this world (as) man upon woman… In eternity there is something else (in) the likeness of mating, yet we call it by these (same) names. (109)

Out of this mystic union becomes a "Son of the Bridal Chamber" (i.e., a "Son of Man"):

If someone becomes (a) Son of the Bridal-Chamber, he shall receive the Light. (143)

The Gospel of Philip proves that, even centuries after Jesus's death, there was a vibrant Christian movement preaching and teaching what Jesus actually taught: the path to union with the Holy Spirit. Surely the only way this could happen is if, during the Apostolic Age, some of Jesus's direct disciples were out there passing on his actual teachings.

A separation of ways must have taken place in the very earliest post-crucifixion days. In one direction went Peter, Paul and faith-based Christianity. In the other direction went those teaching the path of inner spiritual transformation. The likelihood is that this split happened at the very beginning: that there were two different types of disciples left after the death of Jesus. On one hand were those who had been baptized-by-Spirit (or were making progress towards this) and, on the other hand, the rest of the disciples. Jesus's ministry only lasted one or two years so there was not a lot of time for followers to do mountains of inner purification.

"But I tell you truly, there are some standing here who will not taste death until they see the kingdom of God."

- Luke 9:27

This certainly implies that Jesus thought that not all the disciples were going to get there. We would expect then a split in the teachings of the disciples. The ones who had transformed their souls - or believed they would - would continue to teach the inner path. But the ones who were not making progress in transforming their souls would be less committed to preaching it. This second lot would be much more attracted to the idea that there was going to be a Second Coming of Jesus so all they had to do was hang on until then and not have to concern themselves with the narrow hard path of inner spiritual evolution.

The teachings of the mystical apostles didn't win out. Instead Christianity-as-faith was birthed by someone who never even met the living Jesus.

Paul

Paul was no student of Jesus. He hated him posthumously and rabidly persecuted Jews who followed Jesus. But, a couple of years after Jesus's crucifixion, Paul had a revelatory experience. Jesus appeared to him. Instantly Paul was converted to a belief in Jesus and would go on to become a relentless proselytizer for him.

Paul never heard the parables from Jesus's mouth nor did he hear Jesus give the secret knowledge reserved only for his disciples. Any words of Jesus which Paul received, he heard, at best, second-hand. Nevertheless, it was this non-disciple Paul who was to become the founder of a new religion: the faith-based worship of Jesus the Christ.

Paul had no interest in the kingdom of God. Instead Paul's letters to embryonic Christian communities were shaped by nine key beliefs:

1. Jesus was the Son of God

> …the Son of God in power according to the Spirit of holiness by his resurrection from the dead, Jesus Christ our Lord. (Romans 1:4)

2. Jesus died for our sins

> God shows his love for us in that while we were still sinners, Christ died for us. (Romans 5:8)

> …Christ died for our sins… (1 Corinthians 15:3)

3. **Jesus was the Jewish Messiah as foretold in Jewish Scripture.**

> …the Messiah died for our sins in accordance with the Scriptures (1 Corinthians 15:4)[42]

4. **Jesus was raised from the dead as proven by Paul's own and others' sightings of Jesus**

> …Christ… was raised on the third day in accordance with the Scriptures, and that he appeared to Cephas [Peter], then to the twelve. Then he appeared to more than five hundred brothers at one time, most of whom are still alive, though some have fallen asleep [i.e., died]. Then he appeared to James, then to all the apostles. Last of all, as to one untimely born, he appeared also to me. (1 Corinthians 15:3-8)

5. **Very, very soon, there will be a Second Coming with Jesus descending from heaven.**

> For the Lord himself will come down from heaven, with a loud command, with the voice of the archangel and with the trumpet call of God, and the dead in Christ will rise first. After that, we who are still alive and are left will be caught up together with them in the clouds to meet the Lord in the air. And so we will be with the Lord forever. (1 Thessalonians 4:16-17)

6. **Only faith in Jesus can save you at the Second Coming**

> For you yourselves are fully aware that the day of the Lord will come like a thief in the night. While people are saying, "There is peace and security,"

---

[42] Paul wrote in Greek so when referring to "Messiah" he used the word "Christ" (*Christos*). I have changed "Christ" to "Messiah" in this passage to make his point more obvious.

then sudden destruction will come upon them as labor pains come upon a pregnant woman, and they will not escape....

But since we belong to the day, let us be sober, having put on the breastplate of faith and love, and for a helmet the hope of salvation. For God has not destined us for wrath, but to obtain salvation through our Lord Jesus Christ, who died for us so that whether we are awake or asleep [i.e., physically dead] we might live with him. (1 Thessalonians 5:3, 8-10)

7. **Because only faith in Jesus can save us from destruction, Jesus is our Savior**

For many, of whom I have often told you and now tell you even with tears, walk as enemies of the cross of Christ. Their end is destruction, their god is their belly, and they glory in their shame, with minds set on earthly things. But our citizenship is in heaven, and from it we await a Savior, the Lord Jesus Christ, who will transform our lowly body to be like his glorious body, by the power that enables him even to subject all things to himself. (Philippians 3:18-21)

8. **Because faith in Jesus is now the key element in being saved, you don't have to obey the Jewish Law – including such things as men being circumcised.**
This was a key belief of Paul which facilitated the spread of Christianity among Gentiles and empowered Christianity to become a separate religion instead of remaining a Jewish sect.

...we know that a person is not justified by works of the law but through faith in Jesus Christ, so we also have believed in Christ Jesus, in order to be justified by faith in Christ and not by works of the law, because by works of the law no one will be justified. (Galatians 2:16)

> For in Christ Jesus neither circumcision nor uncircumcision counts for anything, but only faith working through love. (Galatians 5:6)

9. The spirit of Jesus is already within all true believers

> And because you are sons, God has sent the Spirit of his Son into our hearts, crying, "Abba! Father!" (Galatians 4:6)

> Or do you not realize this about yourselves that Jesus Christ is in you? (2 Corinthians 13:5)

> I have been crucified with Christ. It is no longer I who live, but Christ who lives in me. (Galatians 2:20)

In Paul's writings, you can see in embryonic form all the key elements which still endure in the Christian religion to this day:

> For God so loved that world that he gave his only begotten Son, Jesus Christ our Lord and Savior who died for our sins, was crucified, dead and buried and rose again on the third day, that whosoever believes in him will not perish but have everlasting life.[43]

And so it was that the writings of Paul became the primary shaper of Christianity through the ages – and not the actual words and teachings of the mystic teacher Jesus of Nazareth.

Where did Paul get these ideas from?

Paul wrote his letters independently of the Gospels. So where did his ideas come from? There are three possible sources:
  1. Experiential

---

[43] See *The Book of Common Prayer* for passages referencing these beliefs. See also John 3:16,18.

2. Word of mouth
3. He made them up or deduced them.

Experiential sources included his own sighting of Jesus, his own inner experiences and the "ecstatic" types of experiences that the early Christians were having: talking in tongues, prophesying, ecstasy. Such experiences gave rise to belief in the resurrection of Jesus and to the belief that the spirit of Jesus was within people (that latter part being understandable in terms of the Imprinting).

Word of mouth would have come second-hand from actual students of Jesus or people who had heard Jesus talk (or claimed to). Paul certainly communicated with one actual disciple of Jesus (Peter) and definitely got some of his ideas from disciples of Jesus (see 1 Corinthians 15:3). But even such word-of-mouth stories were already at risk of contamination: being colored by the attested sightings of Jesus post-crucifixion.

Sightings of Jesus

Reported post-crucifixion sightings of Jesus were arguably the single biggest influence in transforming the teachings of Jesus into the religion of Jesus.

The original version of the Gospel of Mark, the oldest of the Biblical Gospels, actually has no sightings of Jesus. It ends at Mark 16:8 with an empty open tomb. A youth says that Jesus has been raised from the dead and the women run away terrified. This ending leaves open the possibility of sightings of Jesus without saying that they actually happened. It is fascinating that the author of Mark didn't include any sightings of Jesus. The full-on resurrection sightings of Jesus were tacked onto the end of the Gospel of Mark by later writers. Such stories go on to feature prominently as the endings of other Biblical Gospels.

The Biblical accounts of the resurrection contain contradictions which are impossible to reconcile:

In the Gospel of Mark (16:1-8), three women go to the tomb, find the stone already rolled away and, inside the tomb, see a young man dressed in white. This man instructs the women to tell the disciples to go to Galilee where they will see the risen Jesus. The three women run away terrified.

In the Gospel of Matthew (Matt 28), two women go to the tomb. There is a violent earthquake. The stone in front of the tomb has been rolled away and an angel of the Lord is sitting outside on the stone. He instructs the women to tell the disciples to go to Galilee where they will see Jesus. The women hurry away filled not with terror but with joy. Then the women see Jesus who speaks. They clasp his feet and worship him. Eleven disciples then go to Galilee and meet with Jesus on a mountain "to which Jesus had directed them". (There is no account as to how this direction took place.) Some disciples see him and worship him – but some still doubt. Presumably these disciples doubted because they did not see him. There is no ascension.

In the Gospel of Luke (Luke 24), an indeterminate number (but more than three) of "the women who had come with him from Galilee" (Luke 23:55) enter the open tomb. At first, they see no-one but suddenly two men appear and instruct them to tell the disciples that Jesus has risen. This they do. Peter runs to the tomb and sees it empty. That same day Jesus appears to disciples at Emmaus, seven miles from Jerusalem. Later he appears to a group of disciples in Jerusalem. Sometime later, he leads the disciples out to nearby Bethany and ascends to heaven and is not seen again. The same writer, in Acts 1, says that the risen Jesus had hung around for a while "appearing to them during forty days and speaking about the kingdom of God". Nothing of what the risen Jesus said about the kingdom of God in this time is recorded.

In the Gospel of John (John 20-21), one woman only goes out to the tomb (Mary Magdalene) and she sees the stone rolled away. She does not check whether the tomb is empty but runs back to tell Simon Peter and one other disciple that someone has taken the body of Jesus out of the tomb. The two men run to the tomb and see that it is empty and decide that someone has taken the body. Mary Magdalene goes back to the tomb, looks in and now sees two angels who ask her why she is weeping. She turns and sees a man who she thinks is a gardener and he also asks her why she is weeping. When the man says "Mary!" she suddenly recognizes him as Jesus. He tells her not to touch him. That same night he appears to the disciples in a locked room (presumably in Jerusalem). Eight days later, he appears again to convince the doubting Thomas who wasn't there the first time. Later still, he appears a few more times to disciples in Galilee. There is no ascension.

In the letters of Paul, Paul gives the only first-hand account of seeing Jesus after his death. There is no mention of an empty tomb. There is no mention of the risen Jesus saying anything. However, Paul references multiple sightings of Jesus even years after his death (1 Corinthians 15:3-8).

In summary: the resurrection stories are a mess.

There is one important consistency: **Jesus was seen.**

It would be easy indeed for this present book to ignore attested sightings of Jesus. We have already covered everything important about the life of Jesus: the descent of the Holy Spirit (baptism by the Holy Spirit), his teachings about realizing the kingdom of God (baptism by the Holy Spirit), the second mission (suffering and dying), the Transfiguration, the education of God, the Imprinting. It was would be very easy to put post-crucifixion sightings of Jesus into the "don't know, don't care" basket. But there are so many attestations to sightings of Jesus after his death – and the impact of these sightings was so great – that they demand consideration.

The physical resurrection of Jesus's body became one of the key cornerstones of faith-based Christianity. Of course, Jesus is not the only person in the New Testament whose body is allegedly physically resurrected: there was also Lazarus (John 11:1-44) and Jairus's daughter who was either dead or apparently so (Mark 5:21-43). People were also physically raised from the dead in the Old Testament (1 Kings 17:17-24, 2 Kings 4:32-37, 2 Kings 13:21).

If you asked present-day Christians what they think happens after they die, you'd generally get this sort of reply: "The soul departs the body and, if you led a good life and had faith in Jesus as your Savior, your soul goes to heaven. If you didn't, you go to hell." But orthodox Jews back in Jesus's day weren't so big on this. Many Jews tended to a belief in an end-of-days scenario: dead people would "sleep" in their physical bodies and at the end of days, these physical bodies would be resurrected. With this sort of background, one can well understand why, if Jews saw the spiritual body of Jesus, they would be inclined to interpret this as an actual physical resurrection.

Let us put to one side the extraordinarily unlikely idea of the zombie-esque reanimation of Jesus's corpse and look instead at the possibility that Jesus appeared to people in a highly-energized spiritual body – i.e., what people such as Paul saw was the astral body of a physically-deceased Jesus.

Baptism-by-Spirit and the Transfiguration had energized Jesus's spiritual bodies. His astral body would have been vibrant, luminescent. The highly energized astral body of Jesus seems to have lingered near the earthly plane and appeared to the living – even being seen in the daytime.

We actually have one first-hand account of a sighting of Jesus direct – the one from Paul himself. It is hard to question the sincerity of Paul's belief that he saw the figure of Jesus as he turned his whole life upside down on the basis of this sighting. Forget about the blinding flash of light on the road to Damascus – that is from the Acts of the Apostles written by someone else much later. That later writer has three mentions of Paul's conversion experience and they contradict each other. In Acts 9:7, bystanders hear a voice but see nothing and they stay standing. In Act 22:9, they see a light but do not hear a voice. In Acts 26:14, they fall down. Not exactly a masterpiece of consistent recounting. In all three tellings, Paul is blinded by the light and does not see Jesus at all. This is contradicted by Paul's own account in which Jesus appears to him and others:

> For I delivered to you as of first importance what I also received: that Christ died for our sins in accordance with the Scriptures, that he was buried, that he was raised on the third day in accordance with the Scriptures, and that he appeared to Cephas [Peter], then to the twelve. Then he appeared to more than five hundred brothers at one time, most of whom are still alive, though some have fallen asleep. Then he appeared to James, then to all the apostles. Last of all, as to one untimely born, he appeared also to me.
>
> - 1 Corinthians 15:3-8

Paul references over five hundred people having seen Jesus. It is not a small claim. Notice what Paul emphasizes: Jesus "appeared". *He was seen.*

This is the only first-hand account we have. If Jesus had said anything to Paul that this is where he would have recorded it. He would have boasted: "appeared and spoke to me". But he only references Jesus appearing. Moreover, if this vision of Jesus had said something to Paul, then perhaps Paul would have shown much more interest in what Jesus said when he was alive – instead of the almost complete disinterest he shows in the spoken word of Jesus.

We should have very great doubts that, post-crucifixion, the spirit of Jesus said anything to anyone if only because any words which are ascribed to the resurrected Jesus are unbelievably banal and uninteresting. Surely if the miraculously resurrected Jesus had said something, it would have been remembered by all concerned but we have far better evidence for what he said in his life than we do for anything supposedly said after his death.

Also Paul does not mention the resurrected Jesus touching anything or anyone. *Oh, but what about Doubting Thomas, didn't he touch the risen Lord?* No. He was shown the marks and that was enough for him:

> Eight days later, his disciples were inside again, and Thomas was with them. Although the doors were locked, Jesus came and stood among them and said, "Peace be with you." Then he said to Thomas, "Put your finger here, and see my hands; and put out your hand, and place it in my side. Do not disbelieve, but believe." Thomas answered him, "My Lord and my God!"
>
> - John 20:26-28

Thomas never touches Jesus. He just sees and believes.

Across all four Gospels and the letters of Paul, there is only one account that explicitly mentions someone touching Jesus:

And behold, Jesus met them and said, "Greetings!"
And they came up and took hold of his feet and
worshiped him

- Matthew 28:9

One can believe that they may have fell to the ground worshipping the image of Jesus but, if this is the one and only citation of touching, it is just too thin. We are on safe grounds in ruling out any physical touching between the image of Jesus and living human beings.

We are left then with direct and indirect attestations that people saw the image of Jesus. With some of these sightings, the image of Jesus is sufficiently weak or indistinct that many people have trouble recognizing him, including Mary Magdalene (John 20:14), seven disciples fishing (John 21:4) and two disciples walking near Emmaus (Luke 24:13-16). In the Gospel of Matthew (28:16-17), eleven disciples go up a mountain in Galilee to meet with Jesus and some see and believe "but some doubted". The only possible reason for this is that they did not see Jesus – or saw an apparition but did not recognize it as being Jesus.

The image of Jesus suddenly appears from nowhere (Luke 24:36-37), even appearing in rooms where the doors were all shut (John 20:26) and locked (John 20:19).

This is not the behavior of a physical body. It is the behavior of an astral spiritual body.

Paul saw the spirit of Jesus and his conclusion was that the resurrected body is NOT the physical body but rather a spiritual body that looks like the physical body:

> But someone will ask, "How are the dead raised? With what kind of body do they come?" You foolish person! What you sow does not come to life unless it dies. And what you sow is not the body that is to be, but a bare kernel, perhaps of wheat or of some other grain…
> So is it with the resurrection of the dead. What is sown is perishable; what is raised is imperishable. It is sown in dishonor; it is raised in glory. It is sown in weakness; it is raised in power. It is sown

146

> a natural body; it is raised a spiritual body. If there is a natural body, there is also a spiritual body...
>
> I tell you this, brothers: flesh and blood cannot inherit the kingdom of God, nor does the perishable inherit the imperishable. Behold! I tell you a mystery. We shall not all sleep [ie, die], but we shall all be changed, in a moment, in the twinkling of an eye, at the last trumpet. For the trumpet will sound, and the dead will be raised imperishable, and we shall be changed. For this perishable body must put on the imperishable, and this mortal body must put on immortality. When the perishable puts on the imperishable, and the mortal puts on immortality... (1 Corinthians 15:35-37, 42-44, 50-54)

So there you have it from an actual eye-witness: the resurrected body is spiritual not physical.

On the basis of the weight of attestations, here are my conclusions:

1. There is no solid (!) evidence of the reanimation of the physical body of Jesus. The only evidence are reports of an empty tomb. There are certainly alternative explanations as to why a tomb would be empty which are far more likely than the reanimation of a dead body. Also, of course, the reported incidents could well have been fabricated to explain the sightings of Jesus. The extreme inconsistencies between them do tend to indicate fabrication.

2. Baptism by the Holy Spirit and Transfiguration alter the energies of the soul. They energize it. This made Jesus's astral body much more vibrant than any soul has been since. It was even able to appear in daytime.

3. The spiritual body of Jesus was sighted a number of times post-crucifixion. It was a vivid and powerful experience which had a profound effect on some people. The amount of attestations and the effect it had on people who saw the image of Jesus are too compelling to casually dismiss.

4. The vividness of the image varied from sighting to sighting. (Hence the difficulties some had in recognizing it). Again, this bespeaks of an astral body rather than a physical body.

5. Some people seeing the spirit of Jesus may have felt that they received messages from the spiritual realms but there is no reason to believe that the soul of Jesus said anything in the manner that a living body does.

6. Paul's first-hand account of the sightings is pretty sober and constrained – speaking only of Jesus appearing. However, other writers (i.e., the writers of the Gospels of Matthew, Luke and John) blew up the appearances of Jesus's spiritual body by adding flashing lights and special effects: angels, words, ascension, blinding lights, etc.

7. All these sightings were made by Israelites who were not great believers in discarnate souls and so tended to see and believe that the images were those of a resurrected physical body.

The sightings of the spirit of Jesus set in motion a whole chain of beliefs and events:

- The conversion of Paul and preaching of Paul;
- The belief in the physical resurrection of Jesus;
- The belief in the divinity of Jesus;
- The belief that, at the Second Coming of Jesus, the bodies (spiritual and/or physical) of true believers would be resurrected just as Jesus had apparently been;
- The belief that the Second Coming would see the establishment of the kingdom of Jesus on Earth;
- The belief that, as Jesus was divine, faith in him would save you at his Second Coming. He is the Savior.
- The belief that Jesus was the only begotten Son of God.

The idea that Jesus died for our sins

Where did this bizarre idea come from?

Paul was surely the key disseminator of this idea but he says he received it from someone else:

> For I delivered to you as of first importance what
> I also received: that Christ died for our sins in
> accordance with the Scriptures, that he was buried,
> that he was raised on the third day in accordance
> with the Scriptures
>
> - 1 Corinthians 15:3-4

So who thought this idea up?

It needs to be understood that the early Christians were desperate to come up with a reason why Jesus – supposedly the miracle-working Son of God – would allow himself to be crucified. How could Jesus, the divine Messiah, the Christ, a miracle worker, allow himself to be crucified like a common criminal?

Early Christians came up with some very bizarre ideas to explain away how the Son of God would allow himself to be crucified. Here's a sample…

There was a separationist idea which held that the divine separated out from Jesus just before he was crucified. Originally Jesus was just an average bloke. At the River Jordan, at his baptism, a divine entity took possession of Jesus's body and did all the teachings and miracles. Then, just before his crucifixion, the divine entity abandoned the body of flesh, leaving the human Jesus to do all the suffering because the divine can't suffer.

In the second century, Marcion promoted the idea that Jesus was never a real man at all. He just *appeared* to be a man. He was only ever a divine spirit projecting a human image; he was a phantasm. As such, he was never crucified: he just *appeared* to be crucified.

In the first half of the second century, Basilides came up with a cracking idea. Jesus was struggling with carrying his cross on the road to Golgotha so the Romans grabbed a passerby, Simon of Cyrene, and compelled him to help Jesus with the weight of the cross. Jesus took this opportunity to switch the outward appearances of himself and Simon. So that it was really Simon of Cyrene who was crucified and not Jesus; it just looked like Jesus. Meanwhile, Jesus (in the appearance of Simon of Cyrene) was able to stand and laugh at the whole spectacle.[44] That sort of gets around the crucifixion problem but it was obviously damn cruel on the part of Jesus. Certainly, it does not sound like loving your neighbor as yourself. Plus it still means that the divine Jesus had the crap scourged out of him prior to making the switch.

Compared to these out-there ideas, the theory that Jesus allowed himself to be crucified in order to expunge the sins of the world almost starts to sound sane. But there is nothing even vaguely like this idea in the oldest and most reliable of the Gospels, the Gospel of Mark. It starts to creep in with the later Gospels. Consider this passage in Matthew's description of the Last Supper:

> And he took a cup, and when he had given thanks he gave it to them, saying, "Drink of it, all of you, for this is my blood of the covenant, which is poured out for many for the forgiveness of sins."
>
> - Matthew 26:27-28

The phrase "for the forgiveness of sins" is a doctrinally-slanted addition to the original passage in Mark which is simply:

> "This is my blood of the covenant, which is poured out for many."
>
> - Mark 14:24

The Gospel of Luke doesn't make Matthew's doctrinal insertion and is true to the original:

> "This cup that is poured out for you is the new covenant in my blood."
>
> - Luke 22:20

By the time of the Gospel of John, the gloves are off and the whole Gospel is set up to portray Jesus as being the Son of God who has been sent in order to be sacrificed for the forgiveness of sins. In the Gospel of John, the very first person to see Jesus is John the Baptist

---

[44] Virtually all of Basilides actual writings have been lost. This story is attributed to Basilides by a critic, Irenaeus, in *Against Heresies*, Book 1, Chapter 24. www.newadvent.org/fathers/0103124.htm

who immediately announces the Savior by declaring:

> "Behold, the Lamb of God, who takes away the sin
> of the world!"
>
> - John 1:29

Back in those days, at every Passover, every Jewish family (or group of families) was supposed to take a flawless young lamb to the Temple (or, far more likely, purchase one there) in order that it be sacrificed for the forgiveness of their sins and so put them back in right relationship with God. After the priests had killed the lamb in sacrifice, the family or families would go back to the Temple and collect the carcass and roast and eat it that night. All of it had to be consumed before the following morning.

This is how the Gospel of John sets up Jesus from the very beginning: to be the sacrificial Lamb of God so that the sins of the entire world can be forgiven. In line with this, the Gospel of John moves the day of the crucifixion from the day of the Passover (as it is in the Gospel of Mark) to the day before the Passover so that Jesus is crucified and dies at the same time that lambs are being slaughtered at the Temple for the forgiveness of sins.

This Johannine picture gives us clues as to some of the inspiration behind the idea that Jesus died for our sins:

- Jesus died for the benefit of others.
- Jesus died at the Passover.
- Death at the Passover is associated with sacrifices being made for the forgiveness of sin.

Aha!!

Aha!!!

Aha! That is why Jesus died – he died as a Lamb of God, sacrificing himself for the forgiveness of our sins!

This extraordinarily shaky theoretical leap then became enshrined as doctrinal law through the writings of Paul who says he got the idea from someone else: "For I delivered to you as of first importance what I also received: that Christ died for our sins in accordance with the Scriptures…" (1 Corinthians 15:3) This is obviously a ritualized formulation which is passed on to all newcomers to the Jesus movement.

The passage in "Scriptures" that Paul is referring to is Isaiah 53 which contains passages such as:

> because he poured out his soul to death
> and was numbered with the transgressors;
> yet he bore the sin of many

> - Isaiah 53:12.

As noted before, at no time does Isaiah mention the word "Messiah" because he was never predicting a future, suffering Messiah. He was actually talking about the redemption of Israel as a whole. Nevertheless, this conviction that Isaiah was predicting a future, suffering Messiah was pervasive in the Jesus movement and certainly shaped the Gospels.

For instance, as we have seen that, in the Gospel of John (1:29), John the Baptist declares: "Behold, the Lamb of God, who takes away the sin of the world!" This ties in with Isaiah (53:7):

> He was oppressed, and he was afflicted,
> yet he opened not his mouth;
> like a lamb that is led to the slaughter,
> and like a sheep that before its shearers is silent,
> so he opened not his mouth.

The details of this Isaiah "prophecy" were not fulfilled because all the Gospels have Jesus say something during his trial and on the Cross.

Isaiah reads "…he was pierced for our transgressions" (53:5) so the Gospel of John has Jesus's side pierced by a spear. This is not in the other Gospels.

The desire to make Jesus look like the fulfillment of ancient Jewish scripture and "prophecies" certainly shaped Gospel accounts of Jesus's life and his death.

The Gospel with the best claim to be based on reliable word-of-mouth, the Gospel of Mark, makes it plain that the crucifixion was not done for man at all but for God. When Jesus first tells his disciples that he must suffer and die, Peter takes him aside to rebuke him: such a thing must not happen. Jesus replies: "Get behind me, Satan! For you are not setting your mind on the things of God, but on the things of man." So he is doing it not for man but for God.

From inner evolution to faith

Faith.

Christians must have faith.

Salvation comes from having faith in Jesus Christ, our Lord and Savior.

But this is not the message of the Gospels. Across all four Gospels, there are only 29 mentions of "faith" and most of those have to do with whether and why an attempted healing was successful or not.

In the rest of the New Testament (about half of it), there is a massive jump in mentions of "faith" – 199 mentions all up. Paul makes 34 mentions of "faith" in the letter to Romans alone – more than in the entire four Gospels. And the question was not whether to have faith in God – even recalcitrant Jesus-denying Jews did that. The essential thing was to have faith in Jesus.

Much more than its parent religion, Judaism, Christianity made faith the cornerstone of religion. Judaism was more practice-based: you had to keep the Law of Moses and do all the practices – the cleansings, the circumcision, the sacrifices, keeping the Sabbath, etc.

Most of the ancient Mediterranean world was pagan. Pagan religions were all about practice – and mainly about the practice of making sacrifices. Sacrifices were not about getting you into heaven after you died; they were to court the favor of the gods so you could do well in this earthly life. You sacrificed to the appropriate god to get the rain you needed for your crops. You sacrificed to the goddess of love to get that rich man to fall in love with you.

But, with Christians, religion was internal – it was about what you believed in… and you had to believe in Jesus.

Many, many things flowed from this revolutionary emphasis on internal faith. If it was all about faith then you had better get that belief exactly right. This gave rise to a lot of heated debates and polemics about exactly what you should believe. Much of Paul's writings are about this: getting the beliefs right. Get them wrong and Jesus would not save you.

The Christian passion for faith also led to massive persecution of the early Christians. The pagans did not care so much about what people believed. They cared about getting enough rain and that happened by currying favor with the gods but the obdurate Christians would not make sacrifices to the gods because it did not fit in with their "beliefs". Indeed, pagans sometimes described Christians as "atheists" because they did not sacrifice to any god. How could they really believe in this god of theirs if they didn't sacrifice to him?

The Christians were fine while all was well with the world but when something went bad, Christians smelt fishy. There was no rain this season and the crops failed. That meant that the gods were unhappy. *Why were the gods not happy? What did we do that was wrong? It's the Christians! They failed to sacrifice to the gods. The gods are angry with us because the Christians aren't doing the right thing by them. Get the Christians!*

Broadly speaking, violence against Christians was mob-initiated.

When arrested, Christians were generally given a chance by the local ruler to make things right by making a sacrifice to the Emperor or a god. Some Christians did. But many refused and were martyred.

Most pagans were not impressed by the whole Christian thing – new gods were popping in and out of existence all the time, coming and going, seen it all before… been there, believed that. But why won't these obdurate Christians just fulfill their obligations to the rest of us and sacrifice to the gods so that we get our rain? What's so important about this faith stuff anyway?

The Jewish religion escaped this approbation because it was a very ancient religion. Time was on their side. There must be something to this Jewish god simply because the Jews had survived for all this time. Moreover, the Jews made sacrifices to their God. They were okay.

But Christians didn't make any sacrifices. They said they didn't need to. They said that Jesus had done all the sacrificing that was ever necessary. They just needed to have faith in Jesus.

What was all that about? And it couldn't be right anyway. If that was right, where was our rain this year?

Christians said that the rain wasn't important. It was eternal salvation that was important. And that would be theirs through faith in Jesus Christ, their Lord and Savior. This faith sustained them… in life… in death… in martyrdom.

Faith is all you need.

Faith is all you need.

The kingdom of Jesus

Jesus had taught that true inner spiritual evolution – realizing the kingdom of God – is hard; few will stick at it long enough and hard enough to do it.

> "Enter by the narrow gate. For the gate is wide and the way is easy that leads to destruction, and those who enter by it are many. For the gate is narrow and the way is hard that leads to life, and those who find it are few."
>
> - Matthew 7:13-14

But entry to the kingdom of Jesus is not narrow. It is wide: act good and have absolute faith in Jesus – that will take care of everything. That is your salvation.

> …if you confess with your mouth that Jesus is Lord and believe in your heart that God raised him from the dead, you will be saved.
>
> - Romans 10:9

What was the primary aim of every early Pauline Christian? It was to be admitted into the fast-approaching kingdom of Jesus by being judged favorably by Jesus because it was Jesus – not God and certainly not the Son of Man – who would be your judge and jury. Jesus was going to come down from the heavens and appear among the clouds. Then Jesus would judge everyone on the basis of whether they had been good and whether they had faith in him.

> For you may be sure of this, that everyone who is sexually immoral or impure, or who is covetous (that is, an idolater), has no inheritance in the kingdom of Christ and God.
>
> - Ephesians 5:5

Those true believers in Jesus who were asleep (i.e., apparently dead) would first be resurrected from the dead. It had been proven that such a resurrection of the dead can happen because Jesus was resurrected from the dead. He was the first of many. Jesus would gather these resurrected spiritual/physical bodies up into the air and they would immediately followed by the living believers.

This apocalyptic vision may sound strange to the ears of many modern Christians but it was absolutely the key belief of early Pauline-influenced Christian gatherings. And do not think for a minute that the idea of Jesus being an apocalyptic judge is a dead anachronism. This is currently the text of the Roman Catholic mass in English:

> I believe in God,
> the Father almighty,
> Creator of heaven and earth,
> and in Jesus Christ, his only Son, our Lord,
> who was conceived by the Holy Spirit,
> born of the Virgin Mary,
> suffered under Pontius Pilate,
> was crucified, died and was buried;
> he descended into hell;
> on the third day he rose again from the dead;
> he ascended into heaven,
> and is seated at the right hand of God the Father almighty;
> from there he will come to judge the living and the dead.
> I believe in the Holy Spirit,
> the holy catholic Church,
> the communion of saints,
> the forgiveness of sins,
> the resurrection of the body,
> and life everlasting. Amen.

So there you have it – the Pauline doctrine of the kingdom of Jesus complete with an end-of-days apocalypse and bodily resurrection of the dead – still ensconced at the center of Roman Catholic faith.

Pauline doctrines were victorious.

Christianity became and still is about the kingdom of Jesus.

The kingdom of God was vanquished.

Jesus Delusion VII

Paul was a willful man who distorted Jesus's teachings

I would dislike for the previous chapter to be seen as an exercise in Paul-bashing.

Christianity-as-faith started with Paul; and his writings have arguably carried more weight than the actual teachings of Jesus who never sought to start a new religion. For instance, Martin Luther underpinned the entire Protestant Revolution by turning Paul's idea of "saved by faith alone" into a mantra.

Whatever negative influence Paul's epistles have had on the evolution of Christianity-as-faith, he was obviously a sincere and earnest person who promulgated his best understanding. You gain a clearer insight into this if you focus only on the seven letters that are definitely Pauline and eliminate the epistles which most scholars doubt were written by him. (See Appendix Two.)

Paul was writing his letters to gatherings of early Jesus-followers to hold them fast to his version of the truth for a few short years before the Second Coming of Jesus. He was not writing these letters to become part of the canon of an ongoing Christian faith for the next two thousand years.

As I read passages in Paul, I am ineluctably led to consider this question: *Was Paul, to some extent, a mystic? Was Paul part of the way along the seven steps of mysticism as outlined in the Beatitudes?*

Most Christians believe this to be the story of Paul:

- Paul was a fanatical Jew who ruthlessly persecuted Jesus-followers
- Suddenly, unexpectedly, miraculously, Paul had a blinding encounter with the risen Lord Jesus ("blinded by the light")
- Paul instantly became fanatically devoted to Jesus
- Paul immediately began preaching and spreading the word of Jesus across the Mediterranean.

In this, Christians are following the story of Paul as told in Acts - except that this is not the story which Paul himself tells. According to him, after his encounter with Jesus, he went to Arabia for as much as three years with no mention of any preaching in this time. This area of the world is more associated with early mystic Christianity than anywhere else. Consider that the Nag Hammadi Library was discovered in Egypt. Paul actually boasts about how little contact he had with disciples of the historical Jesus:

> I want you to know, brothers and sisters, that the gospel I preached is not of human origin. I did not receive it from any man, nor was I taught it; rather, I received it by revelation from Jesus Christ. For you have heard of my previous way of life in Judaism, how intensely I persecuted the church of God and tried to destroy it. I was advancing in Judaism beyond many of my own age among my people and was extremely zealous for the traditions of my fathers. But when God, who set me apart from my mother's womb and called me by his grace, was pleased to reveal his Son in me so that I might preach him among the Gentiles, my immediate response was not to consult any human being. I did not go up to Jerusalem to see those who were apostles before I was, but I went into Arabia. Later I returned to Damascus.
>
> Then after three years, I went up to Jerusalem to get acquainted with Cephas [Peter] and stayed with him fifteen days. I saw none of the other apostles—only James, the Lord's brother. I assure you before God that what I am writing you is no lie.
>
> Then I went to Syria and Cilicia. I was personally unknown to the churches of Judea that are in Christ. They only heard the report: "The man who formerly persecuted us is now preaching the faith he once tried to destroy." And they praised God because of me. (Galatians 1:11-24)

In Second Corinthians, Paul relates a mystical experience from this period in his life in Arabia, ascribing it to "a man in Christ":

> I must go on boasting. Though there is nothing to
> be gained by it, I will go on to visions and
> revelations of the Lord. I know a man in Christ
> who fourteen years ago was caught up to the third
> heaven—whether in the body or out of the body I
> do not know, God knows. And I know that this
> man was caught up into paradise—whether in the
> body or out of the body I do not know, God
> knows— and he heard things that cannot be told,
> which man may not utter. (2 Corinthians 12:1-4)

This certainly sounds like an experience from stage five of the mystic path, the stage of visions: "Blessed are the pure in heart for they shall see God." Perhaps Paul also had visions of the face of Jesus:

> For God, who said, "Let light shine out of
> darkness," has shone in our hearts to give the light
> of the knowledge of the glory of God in the face
> of Jesus Christ. (2 Corinthians 4:6).

One has to conclude that Paul spent years in inner contemplation or inner work. In many places, Paul indicates that he has had experiences of an inner connection with Jesus and he expects other Jesus-followers to experience likewise:

> Or do you not realize this about yourselves, that
> Jesus Christ is in you? (2 Corinthians 13:5)

> And because you are sons, God has sent the Spirit
> of his Son into our hearts, crying, "Abba! Father!"
> (Galatians 4:6)

> Do you not know that your bodies are members of
> Christ? (1 Corinthians 6:15)

> But he who is joined to the Lord becomes one
> spirit with him (1 Corinthians 6:17)

Paul also indicates that this inner connection with Jesus is a connection with him on the cross and in his death:

> We know that our old self was crucified with him... (Romans 6:6)

> I have been crucified with Christ. It is no longer I who live, but Christ who lives in me. (Galatians 2:20)

> Do you not know that all of us who have been baptized into Christ Jesus were baptized into his death? (Romans 6:3)

Paul also draws a close connection between Christ and (the Holy) Spirit:

> Now the Lord is the Spirit... (2 Corinthians 3:17)

> For just as the body is one and has many members, and all the members of the body, though many, are one body, so it is with Christ. For in one Spirit we were all baptized into one body – Jews or Greeks, slaves or free – and all were made to drink of one Spirit. (1 Corinthians 12:12-13)

These sorts of experiences are congruent with the experiences of Christian mystics in subsequent ages.

So the story of Paul is not a-sighting-of-the-risen-Jesus-creates-instant-preacher. Rather the initial sighting seems to have sparked Paul to go on an inner journey and that journey convinced him that he had an inner connection with Jesus. Such revelations empowered him to preach Jesus to the Gentiles. It seems that Paul did years of inner spiritual work that took him as far as stage five on the path of blessedness ("Blessed are the pure in heart for they shall see God" – i.e., have spiritual visions) but he seems to have stopped at this stage with the concomitant dangers of misunderstanding this as the endpoint of the path.

A further critical question is: When and how did Paul become so convinced of a Second Coming of Jesus?

Obviously crucial was seeing Jesus on the road to Damascus. Doubtless also influential were his inner experiences of Jesus the

Christ. Perhaps pivotal were those fifteen days he spent with the Apostle Peter just before he started on his ministry. Perhaps that is when his belief in a Second Coming was formulated. If he had been convinced of an imminent forthcoming Second Coming of Jesus prior to meeting with Peter, why did he spend years in Arabia and Damascus when he could have been out there spreading the urgent word?

Let us close out our discussion of Paul by reminding ourselves how earnest Paul was and how unlikely was the survival and lightning growth of the Jesus movement:

> Are they servants of Christ? I am a better one—I am talking like a madman—with far greater labors, far more imprisonments, with countless beatings, and often near death. Five times I received at the hands of the Jews the forty lashes less one. Three times I was beaten with rods. Once I was stoned. (2 Corinthians 11:23-25.)

The Last Jesus Delusion

The (understandable) delusion of Christian mystics

As we approach the end of two books – *The Jesus Code* and *The Crucifixion Code* – we are in a position to broach the final mystery of these books: these books.

Why has it taken two thousand years for someone to mount a serious case that Jesus was a mystic? How could there not be another book out there mounting a serious, systematic case that the historical Jesus was a mystic?

???

Here is my explanation...

In one corner, we have faith-based Christians, including theologians and Church "leaders". The doctrines of their faith are not primarily a product of the teachings of Jesus; rather, they mainly owe their heritage to the teachings of Paul. Any faint inner awareness such Christians have of the Imprint of Jesus is just taken as proof that he was the Son of God for all eternity and confirms them in the blindness of their faith.

In the second corner, we have a comparatively recent entry into the ring: serious academic historians. They genuinely want to get at the historical Jesus but they have no background in mysticism – no experiential background and, in the vast majority of cases, no academic interest in the subject. It seems to have simply not occurred to them that Jesus could have been a mystic and that his teachings about the kingdom of God could be a reference to something that emerges on the mystic path. Since Albert Schweitzer's brilliant 1906 book, *The Quest of the Historical Jesus*, most academics have attached themselves to the idea that Jesus was a failed apocalyptic Jewish preacher and rarely stray from their devotion to that path.

In the third corner, we have Christian mystics. We have the Meister Eckharts, the St Teresas of Avila, the St Gregorys of Palamas and all the other less eloquent Christian mystics and the many silent ones. But they too have major blind spots. Most of them never knew that there were mystics in other spiritual traditions: Hindu mystics,

Muslim mystics, pagan mystics. As far as they knew, there could only be Christian mystics. Moreover, their inner experiences included visions of Jesus. Such visions just confirmed to them that Jesus was indeed the Son of God. It never occurred to them that Jesus may have been another mystic like them.

And, in the fourth and final corner, standing very much apart, we have two books – *The Jesus Code* and *The Crucifixion Code*.

By this stage, you will have already formed a strong opinion about my books – for better or for worse. It is not my place here to argue for their uniqueness but just to express my ongoing shock that they do seem to be so unique.

Part Last

Jesus Now

"But who do you say that I am?"

- Mark 8:29

The endpoint of the quest for the historical Jesus

The historical Jesus was not "the only begotten Son of God". He was not "the Messiah". And he never believed he was either of those things. Nor did he claim to be them.

Jesus was Jewish and never sought to start a new religion, more-or-less be worshipped. He was a normal man who sought greater meaning in life. In pursuit of this quest, he became the student of a mystic, a mystic, and a teacher of the mystic path.

Like his teacher, he believed that this momentous new spiritual phenomenon – seemingly brand new – signaled that God the Father wanted to harvest the souls who could bear fruit and discard the ones who showed no promise.

This picture gives us back a Jesus that we have lacked for two thousand years. It gives us back a humble, rational man: a man who was clear-minded enough not to believe that he was the foretold Messiah. He never entertained the absurd idea that he was a different sort of Messiah – the Messiah-you-have-when-your-not-having-a-Messiah.

It never occurred to Jesus that he was the only begotten Son of God. He clearly always rated his teacher, John the Baptist, as greater than himself for John had pioneered the mystic path for Israelites. How could Jesus have entertained the idea that he was the only begotten Son of God when he rated John the Baptist as greater than himself?

He was not the deluded, failed apocalyptic preacher that academics have so long believed. Whatever reckoning of souls Jesus believed in, he believed in for a reason. When some experience led him to the belief that the soul of his teacher, the "Son of Man", would return to lead an apocalyptic intervention on the Earth, he did not wildly declare this to the general public but kept it as a private sharing with his disciples.

From Jesus's own inner path, things developed that could have never been foreseen when he first set his face towards the wilderness: being singled out by God to suffer on his behalf, the Transfiguration, crucifixion, the Imprinting.

Jesus was an obscure hick preacher from a one-donkey town in a backwater country of the Roman Empire… who would posthumously become the most famous and impactful person in the history of planet Earth. This is the single most extraordinary chain of events in human history. The explanation of this was always going to be beyond the bounds of the ordinary.

> Just as the crusaders [looking for Jesus at the tomb] could not find the Christ because they did not seek him within themselves, contemporary crusaders cannot find Christ Jesus because they do not seek him with the powers that lie within the human soul.
>
> - Rudolf Steiner, "Christ's path through the centuries", Lecture Five in *Approaching the Mystery of Golgotha*

Jesus, Man, Son of Man

When you see films about Jesus, he often comes across as a feminized, almost androgynous figure: a virgin who was the product of a virgin birth.

He was nothing like this.

He was deep into adulthood before he found his way to John the Baptist and started on his path of inner transformation. The chances of his being a virgin are almost as remote as the chances of his being born of a virgin.

He was a man's man. A real human man. Flesh and blood. He pissed; he farted; he shat.

He was a construction worker who worked with his hands. Very probably he was illiterate. If he was alive now he'd be a beer-drinker – back then he drank wine (Matt 11:18-19). He wasn't fussy about washing hands before eating (Mark 7:1-23). He got fed up and angry sometimes (Mark 3:5). Two Gospels record him as crying (Luke 19:41; John 11:35). He complained that people didn't give credence to what he said, that they didn't listen (Mark 9:19; Matt 11:20-24). He pleaded not to be tortured to death (Mark 14:32-39).

He was a human being. An Average Jo. But he became extraordinary through his inner work that opened up his soul to divine possibilities and so became the central player in the evolution of the spiritual universe.

And you, likewise, have these sorts of possibilities within you.

The Death of Covenants

Obey the Ten Commandments and the Law of Moses; and, in return, the Lord God will look after the Israelite nation. That was the Old Covenant of the Israelites.

John the Baptist and Jesus infuriated the Jewish hierarchy because they said that this covenant was dead – or at least superseded. They preached a New Covenant: *Evolve your soul, realize the kingdom of God, bear fruit for God then your soul will be saved; and, in return, God will act to wipe out the evil and irredeemable souls.*

That covenant died on the Cross with Jesus's scream: "*Eloi, Eloi, lema sabachthani!?*"

Just as John the Baptist and Jesus infuriated the religious establishment of their day by their denial of the Old Covenant, so too this book may well infuriate many Christians by its denial of "the Christian covenant". Faith-based Christians believe that they have a covenant with God: *Have faith in Jesus as my Savior and act good and then, when I die, I will go to heaven.* This book says, "No." This is simply not in alignment with what Jesus taught, with what Jesus wanted people to do, and with the realities of the actual spiritual path. It is a post-crucifixion invention.

Covenants are comforting. People wrap themselves in covenants, comforting themselves that this covenant guarantees them a meaningful life and a meaningful afterlife. Pointing out that the emperor has no clothes – that there is no covenant – generally not a popular activity.

Many Jews still believe in the old covenant of Moses.

Many Christians will doubtless still cling to their covenant even though this book has proven that it is out of alignment with the teachings of Jesus.

Muslims too have their covenant: believing that if they follow the Qur'an and believe that there is One God and Mohammed is his prophet, they will end up in a fleshy paradise replete with virgins.

Atheists have their covenant: *If I have faith that "Science" is the One True Knowledge, that makes me smarter than all the silly people who believe in religion and spirituality, and therefore, my life is more meaningful and genuine than theirs.*

Many people now seem to have faith that in a covenant with life: *If I act good, work hard and have a family, my life must have meaning.*

How's that working out?

Presently there is only one spiritual covenant and it is a question: *You will die. The only thing that can survive that death is your soul. Life gives you the opportunity to heal and evolve your soul. What are you going to do with that opportunity?*

An ass which turns a millstone did a hundred miles walking. When it was loosed, it found that it was still at the same place.

- Gospel of Philip 56

Don't let this be your life.

Appendices

Appendix One

Next… a translation issue

Apart from a few Aramaic phrases, the Biblical Gospels were originally written in Greek.

Older translations into English such as the King James Version were executed by true believers certain that Jesus was the Messiah and the Son of God.

In 1988, non-religious scholars set out to write a fresh translation, *The Complete Gospels*. But they did not set out to write a neutral translation. Rather, they assumed the correctness of the received academic view of Jesus – that he was a deluded apocalyptic prophet – and they adjusted their translation accordingly. See *The Complete Gospels*, p. 12, where it is admitted that their translation of "*Basileia tou Theo*" (the kingdom of God) was rendered as "God's imperial rule" to fit in with an apocalyptic view of Jesus's teachings. The politest thing I could say about this translation is that it is awkward. I actually think that it is unforgivably horrendous.

There has never been a translation in which the translator took into account even the possibility that Jesus was a mystic teaching the path of inner transformation. In writing these two books on Jesus and his life, I have been inconvenienced by my inability to read the New Testament in its original Greek. Fortunately there are many frank discussions of Bible translations widely available so I have been able to study the issues and the alternatives.

Also bear in mind that Jesus spoke in Aramaic so, even if you could read the original New Testament Greek, at best, you are still reading a translation of what Jesus originally said.

The issue of translation comes into sharp focus with John the Baptist's enigmatic question carried out to the preaching Jesus. This question has been traditionally translated as: "Are you the one who is to come, or shall we look for another?" (Matthew 11:3). This translation has been favored by both true believers and academics because they think they can make a case that John's question is an oblique reference to a Messiah *who is to come*. But, if Messiah-ship was the issue in John's mind, then why didn't he simply ask: "Are you the Messiah?"

Consider this parallel. You live in a village and, for several days on end, passers-by tell you: "There is a two-headed man coming." (Consider Siamese twins.) When the two-headed man arrives in the village and is standing in front of you, you don't say: "Ahh, you are the one who is to come'. You say: "Oh, you're the two-headed man everyone's been talking about."

When the disciple Peter claimed that Jesus was the Messiah (Mark 8:29), he didn't look at Jesus and say: "You are the one who is to come!"

The argument that John's question was a bent way of asking whether Jesus was the Messiah is thin to the point of anorexic. Yet it is also understandable because until now people have not had an alternative way of making sense of John's enigmatic question.

The key Greek word in this passage is ἔρχομαι *(erchomai)* and that word has other translations besides "come". It can, for instance, be translated as "arise". "Are you the one who is to arise or shall we look for another?" This gives it a completely different sense.

It can also be translated as "come after" or "next".[45] *"Are you the one who is to be next or shall we look for another?"* It is this translation which I use. The arguments I make about what John the Baptist was asking about hold up just as strongly with the translation of "arise". Indeed, the arguments stand up even under the traditional translation but less elegantly.

This questioning of the status of Jesus by John the Baptist is extraordinarily anomalous – so anomalous that it must surely be historically accurate. This incident is simply not one that a true believer in Jesus would make up. The reason that it is so out-there anomalous is because the Gospels go to ridiculous lengths to portray John the Baptist as acknowledging the superiority of Jesus before he has even met him (Mark 1:7-8; Matthew 1:11-12; Luke 3:15-17; John 1:26). So why would John the Baptist later be questioning Jesus's status??

This incident is so embarrassingly anomalous that the authors of *Killing Jesus* (pp. 98-99), Bill O'Reilly and Martin Dugard, try to explain it away as John the Baptist having gone stir-crazy in prison. I have put

---

[45] See, for instance, these discussions:
  biblestudytools.com/ lexicons/greek nas/erchomai.html;
  blueletterbible.org/lang/Lexicon/Lexicon.cfm?strongs=G2064&t=ESV

forward a much more coherent and revealing explanation that does not involve insanity.

Appendix Two

Sources

Hereinafter follow comments on the sources which I have drawn upon. If you wish to know more about particular sources, I would suggest you start by checking out the relevant entry in Wikipedia. If you want more depth after that, I recommend the well-written books of Bart D. Ehrman (see Bibliography).

Historicity

When it comes to understanding the historical Jesus, we are not blessed with written accounts from the man himself nor even writings which can be reliably attributed to eyewitnesses. Instead there were oral traditions which, years or decades after the death of Jesus, were written down in Greek. Jesus himself would have spoken Aramaic.

As in all historical assessments, there is a rule of thumb that, all other things being equal, earlier sources are better sources. For instance, the Gospel of Mark was written decades before the Gospel of John. This in itself lends the Gospel of Mark a greater measure of credence as a record of the life and words of the historical Jesus.

When New Testament scholars seek to evaluate the historical reliability of a passage about Jesus, they use three main criteria:

1. The criterion of independent attestation.

Does the event appear independently in more than one source? If it does, then this gives it more weight to be considered to be historically accurate – just as, at a modern-day legal trial, several eyewitnesses independently agreeing in their accounts is more compelling than one.

The following sources are considered to be independent:

- The Gospel of Mark
- The Gospel of John
- The Gospel of Thomas
- "Q"
- "L"

- "M"
- The letters of Paul

(See below for discussion of these sources.)

If all or almost all of these independently refer to some event then this gives independent attestation of the event. This is true, for instance, both of the crucifixion and Jesus going out to be baptized by John the Baptist which are referenced in all sources. Of course, it is perfectly possible that some event may have happened but only have been attested to in one source. Nevertheless, independent attestation does lend greater weight to its likelihood.

2. The criterion of dissimilarity

Is this something that a true believer in Jesus would be likely to make up or is it *dissimilar* to something that a true believer would want in there but, nevertheless, it IS in there?

For instance, in the Gospel of Matthew 11:11, Jesus says, "Truly, I say to you, among those born of women there has arisen no one greater than John the Baptist." This is Jesus placing John the Baptist equal to or above himself and so it is extraordinarily dissimilar to what a faith-based Gospel-writer would invent. This gives this passage significant brownie points to be considered as historically accurate.

3. The criterion of contextual credibility

Is this something that would have or could have happened in first-century Palestine?

This criterion arguably counts against significant slabs of the Gospel of John. How Jesus talks in this Gospel just does not ring true to how a country preacher in 1st Century Palestine would talk. By contrast, how Jesus talks in the Gospel of Mark has significantly more contextual credibility.

One example of contextual credibility is the appearance of Aramaic phrases. The Gospels were originally written in Greek but Jesus would have spoken Aramaic. The multiple appearances of Aramaic phrases in the Gospel of Mark lend contextual credibility.

Biblical Sources

Jesus spoke Aramaic but, apart from a handful of Aramaic phrases, the Biblical Gospels were written in Greek because, back then, Greek was the "lingua Franca" of the Mediterranean. Greek was the equivalent to what English is today. Even the Hebrew Bible (i.e., the "Old Testament") was then mainly being read in Greek and not Hebrew. Greek was widespread because of the conquests by Alexander the Great and his vision of uniting nations into one world.

The attribution of a particular Gospel to a particular disciple such as "Mark" or "Matthew" is, let us say, "honorific". We don't know for certain who wrote them.

The first three Gospels – Mark, Matthew and Luke – are referred to as the "Synoptic Gospels" because they are, largely, in sync and can be "seen together" (syn-optic). By contrast, the Gospel of John is wildly different.

In places, the Gospels contradict each other. A few of many examples:

- The Gospel of Mark has Jesus crucified on the day of the Passover; the Gospel of John has him crucified on the day before the Passover.
- In the Gospels of Mark and Matthew, Jesus does not start preaching until after the arrest of John the Baptist. In the Gospel of John, Jesus is preaching prior to John the Baptist's arrest.
- The Gospel of Luke and the Gospel of Matthew both have nativity accounts but they are almost entirely different. In Matthew, after the birth, Joseph and Mary flee to Egypt. In Luke, they return to Nazareth. What most people think of as Jesus's nativity is an amalgam of the two.
- The Gospels of Luke and Matthew both list Jesus's family tree but they are radically different.

I do not read Greek so I have been dependent on translations by others and reading discussions of alternative translations. I have generally used the translation of the English Standard Version except where specified. The other translations I draw on are the International Standard Version (ISV), the New International Version (NIV), English Revised Edition (ERE), the King James Version (KJV), and R.J. Miller (ed), *The Complete Gospels.* I have no compunction about picking and choosing between different translations as there is no such thing as a definitive translation. Moreover, this book has been executed at a huge disadvantage. Many translations of the Gospels have been slanted by the translator's belief that Jesus was the only begotten son of God for all eternity. At the other end of the spectrum, the translations in R.J. Miller (ed), *The Complete Gospels,* are slanted by an assumption of the correctness of the academic view of Jesus – that he was a failed apocalyptic preacher. See *The Complete Gospels,* p. 12, where it is admitted that their translation of *"Basileia tou Theo"* (the kingdom of God) was rendered as "God's imperial rule" to fit in with an apocalyptic view of Jesus's teachings.

There has *never* been a translation of the Gospels empathetic to the ideas in this book – that Jesus was a mystic teaching the path of inner transformation. One of my hopes is that, in the wake of this book, a Greek scholar will do such a translation. It would be more than intriguing to see what emerges.

I have generally rendered the Greek word "Christos" into its Jewish form of "Messiah" as this gives it a more valid historical flavor.

biblehub.com is a great resource for comparing translations.

The Dating of the Biblical Gospels

Christianity was initially spread by word of mouth – not surprising in a world where something like 97% of the world was illiterate.

Compounding this, one of the primary spreaders of the Jesus movement was the Apostle Paul who preached that a Second Coming of Jesus was going to happen any day now. As such, the point of writing stuff down for one's children and one's children's children – not that great. Paul never met the living Jesus or heard him speak so he was not well equipped to spread the actual teachings of Jesus.

Sooner or later, a few key individuals started writing the oral tradition down.

There is a very broad consensus that the Gospel of John was the last Gospel written, probably somewhere around the end of the first Century. The Jesus in this Gospel is very remote from the earthy parable-preacher of the three Synoptic Gospels.

The Synoptic Gospels are considered by academics to have been written down in this order: Mark, Matthew, Luke. One of the major reasons for this ordering is that both Matthew and Luke draw heavily on the Gospel of Mark. Luke actually admits that he is writing a composite Gospel drawing on previous writings (Luke 1:1-4).

A common academic dating for the Synoptic Gospels is something like this:

- The Gospel of Mark 70 A.D.
- The Gospel of Matthew 80 A.D.
- The Gospel of Luke 80-90 A.D.

This would mean that the first Gospel, Mark, was written down around 40 years after the death of Jesus.

I believe that these datings for the Synoptic Gospels are far too late.

There is actually a Gospel which more-or-less dates itself. This is the Gospel of Luke. The author of this also wrote the Acts of the Apostles. Together they comprise around a quarter of the New Testament. It is a sprawling narrative often referred to by scholars as Luke-Acts. Acts of the Apostles ends with the Apostle Paul living in Rome awaiting trial – a trial which would culminate in his execution. There is no reason why Acts would end at this point unless this was actually the state of affairs at the time the author finished writing. If Paul had already been martyred for his faith, the author would have put it in the Gospel, boasting about how he'd died in the name of Jesus. But he didn't record this. This would date the writing of Acts (and therefore the writing of the Gospel of Luke) at around 61 A.D.

In this case, the Gospel of Mark would have had to have been written before 61 A.D. – possibly decades before that. The academic dating of the Gospel of Mark at 70 A.D. seems to be based on one solitary passage:

> And as he came out of the temple, one of his disciples said to him, "Look, Teacher, what wonderful stones and what wonderful buildings!" And Jesus said to him, "Do you see these great buildings? There will not be left here one stone upon another that will not be thrown down."
>
> - Mark 13:1-2

The academic reasoning seems to be this: *Ah, this was Jesus "predicting" the destruction of the Temple in Jerusalem but this only happened in 70 A.D. when the Romans sacked the city. Therefore, the Gospel of Mark was written after the destruction of the Temple or when this destruction seemed inevitable. So this "prediction" was never said by the historical Jesus but was written into Jesus's mouth by Mark to make it look like Jesus made an accurate prediction.*

I absolutely do not understand why this is seen as a "prediction" at all. This is the classic way mystics teach students. Far and away, the most gob-smacking physical thing that the disciples would ever see in their entire lives was the Second Temple in Jerusalem. It was like the Vatican, the Taj Mahal and the Sydney Opera House all rolled up into one. In response to his disciples' awe, Jesus says: "*Yes, yes. All very impressive but it is ephemeral. It will all pass.*" *Everything physical passes away. Only things of the spirit endure. The evolution of the soul is the only way to build your house upon a rock that will forever endure* (see Matthew 7:24-27).

Moreover, if the author of the Gospel of Mark was writing in 70 A.D. and wanted to put successful predictions into the mouth of Jesus, he could have put a lot more predictions in than just this solitary one. He could have put in predictions involving Jewish rebellion and short-term triumphs and the revenge of Rome. This was no prediction by Jesus. It was simply a mystic teacher pointing out the ephemeral nature of the physical.

On this basis then, the Gospel of Mark could be dated decades earlier than the traditional academic dating; and that means that the Gospels of Matthew and Luke could have also been written decades earlier than the traditional datings.

The Gospel of Mark could have easily been written down in 40 A.D. or even earlier.

We can also draw an illuminating contrast between the Gospel of Mark and the Gospel of John. That later Gospel, written so very many decades after the death of Jesus, eliminated any incident or saying that did not support the idea that Jesus was the Son of God. If the Gospel of Mark was written four decades after the death of Jesus, isn't that also what would have happened? Any discomforting passages in the oral tradition would have been culled? Instead, there are many many things in the Gospel of Mark which are dissimilar to what a Jesus follower would want to hear. Just a few of many, many examples:

- Jesus's mother and brothers thinking he had totally lost the plot by starting to preach (Mark 3:21)

- Jesus being rejected by his hometown (Mark 6:1-6)
- Jesus failing to heal people (Mark 6:5)
- The Transfiguration - which makes no sense for someone who was already the Son of God (Mark 9:2-8)
- Jesus calling out on the Cross: "My God, my God, why hast thou forsaken me?" (Mark 15:34)
- The naked man: this being the most bizarre incident in the entire Gospel of Mark; one that no-one has an explanation for and which was deleted from subsequent Gospels. After Jesus is arrested in the Garden of Gethsemane and as he is being led away for trial, the following incident is recorded: "And a young man followed him, with nothing but a linen cloth about his body. And they seized him, but he left the linen cloth and ran away naked." (Mark 14:51-52)

Given passages which are so dissimilar to what Jesus followers would want to hear or would ever make up, the onus is on the academics who want to date the Synoptic Gospels so late (70 A.D. or later) to make a comprehensively convincing case. They haven't. The case that all three Synoptic Gospels were written before the execution of Paul is stronger.

As such, the Gospel of Mark may have been written only a handful of years after the death of Jesus. A final strong piece of evidence for this is that, despite being written in Greek, the Gospel of Mark features dramatic Aramaic words and phrases. Surely Aramaic phrases would have been one of the things most likely to be eroded away and discarded over time.

The Gospel of Mark

The Gospel of Mark is the earliest of the four Biblical Gospels. It has a very appealing, minimalist, bare-bones feel to it. The Gospel of Mark is virtually universally considered by Biblical scholars to be the earliest and most reliable source for events in Jesus's life. By contrast, The Gospel of Thomas and "Q" (see below) are sayings gospels. They contain few biographical details but have significant credibility as containing things that Jesus said – or being close to what he said.

The Gospel of Mark has no nativity scenes and starts with the figure of John the Baptist.

Scholars agree that the actual Gospel of Mark ended at 16:8. Women go to the tomb of Jesus, find it empty, and a young man sitting there. They run away terrified. Subsequent scenes of disciples talking to a risen Jesus were tacked on the end of the Gospel of Mark by later writers.

There is an identifiable tension in the Gospel of Mark between the author's dedication to getting the details of Jesus's life and teachings accurate on one hand and, on the other hand, making points about Jesus that Jesus-followers believed and wanted to hear. Some examples of this tension:

1. **Jesus was superior to John the Baptist even though Jesus never said so**
   So he puts the words that Jesus was superior into the mouth of John the Baptist (Mark 1:7-8).

2. **Jesus was the Son of God even though he never said so**
   So, amazingly, Mark puts the words claiming that Jesus is the Son of God into the mouths of people possessed by impure spirits (Mark 3:10-12) and a Gentile Roman soldier at Jesus's crucifixion (Mark 15:37-39)!

3. **Jesus was the Jewish Messiah even though he never said so**
   So, instead, the claim that Jesus was the Messiah comes out of the mouth of the disciple Peter (Mark 8:29).

4. **Jesus could have risen after three days**
   Fascinatingly, the author of the Gospel of Mark records no incidents where the risen Jesus is seen; but, as Mark knows that such stories are rife, he has the story of an empty tomb so that at least allows for the possibility of a risen Jesus:

   > When the Sabbath was past, Mary Magdalene, Mary the mother of James, and Salome bought spices, so that they might go and anoint him. And very early on the first day of the week, when the sun had risen, they went to the tomb. And they were saying to one another, "Who will roll away the stone for us from the entrance of the tomb?" And looking up, they saw that the stone had been

rolled back – it was very large. And entering the tomb, they saw a young man sitting on the right side, dressed in a white robe, and they were alarmed. And he said to them, "Do not be alarmed. You seek Jesus of Nazareth, who was crucified. He has risen; he is not here. See the place where they laid him. But go, tell his disciples and Peter that he is going before you to Galilee. There you will see him, just as he told you." And they went out and fled from the tomb, for trembling and astonishment had seized them, and they said nothing to anyone, for they were afraid.

- Mark 16:1-8

The most puzzling part of this is at the end: "…and they said nothing to anyone, for they were afraid". If they said nothing to anyone, how did anyone else ever find out about it? How did Mark, the author of this Gospel, ever find out about it?

Speculation: Is this Mark making up an excuse for why he'd never heard a story about an empty tomb from a reliable source – but, nevertheless, had to put the story in to allow the possibility of sightings of a resurrected Jesus?

5. The Apocalypse will be very apocalyptic

The Jesus-followers around this time must have been extremely dedicated to the belief in a forthcoming apocalypse because this is the subject where Mark's dedication to capturing the actual words of Jesus seems to be thrown out the window. The Gospel of Mark (13:3-37) has an amazingly long Jesus monologue on a forthcoming apocalypse – a monologue so long that no-one could possibly have recalled it verbatim. This is not to say that Jesus never said anything apocalyptic, but it does seem likely that the author of Mark threw in everything he had and then some into this speech.

*

The Greek in the Gospel of Mark is apparently fairly low-class and was often "enhanced" by the writers of the Gospels of Matthew and Luke. They also took it upon themselves to fill in perceived gaps. This seems to especially be the case with the Gospel of Matthew. The following is one example of Matthew adding to the Gospel of Mark. It occurs just after Jesus informs his disciples that he must suffer and die.

The original Markan version:

> And Peter took him aside and began to rebuke him. But turning and seeing his disciples, he rebuked Peter and said, "Get behind me, Satan! For you are not setting your mind on the things of God, but on the things of man."
>
> - Mark 8:32-33.

Behold the embellishment in the Gospel of Matthew:

> And Peter took him aside and began to rebuke him, saying, "Far be it from you, Lord! This shall never happen to you." But he turned and said to Peter, "Get behind me, Satan! You are a hindrance to me. For you are not setting your mind on the things of God, but on the things of man."
>
> - Matthew 16:22-23

This is pretty obviously an imaginative Matthew fill-in. If Peter took Jesus aside, it would be because he did not want anyone to hear what he was going to say to Jesus. So who heard and recorded this (apart from Peter)? By contrast, bystanders would have heard Jesus's strong reply. The author of the Gospel of Matthew has surely written words into Peter's mouth.

In understanding the relationship of Mark to the other synoptic Gospels of Matthew and Luke, it should be kept in mind that Luke and Matthew had access to much earlier versions of Mark than we do. Because of this, it is possible that some of the passages of the Gospel of Luke or Matthew are more like the original words of Mark than the version of Mark that has survived into the present. This becomes more compelling when Luke and Matthew render a passage of Mark in an identical way, but the passage is rendered differently in Mark. For instance, when Jesus is undergoing a grilling by the high priests, they ask him if he is the Son of the Blessed One. In Mark 14:62, the answer is "I am". In both Matthew and Luke, the equivalent answer is much vaguer. In Matthew, it is "You have said so" (26:64); in Luke, it is "You say that I am." (22:70). It is possible but *highly unlikely* that both Matthew and Luke coincidentally changed the very direct reply in Mark into something vaguer. But they would have no reason to do so. The other alternative is that they accurately rendered the original version of Mark and the version of Mark that we now have been altered to the more absolute: "I am". Certainly, a faith-based Christian scribe would have a vested interest in changing Jesus's reply to the less ambivalent "I am". Or, indeed, there could have been an accidental omission of a few words.

Q (50 AD? Possibly earlier)

"Q" stands for "Quelle" which is German for "source". An independent copy of Q has never been found. It has been reconstructed by extracting out the passages in Luke and Matthew that are virtually identical but not found in the Gospel of Mark. You can find an attempted reconstruction of "Q" in Robert J. Miller (ed), *The Complete Gospels*.

Q is almost entirely a sayings gospel recording things that Jesus allegedly said.

Nowhere in Q is it intimated that Jesus was the Messiah or the Son of God. This is a powerful indicator that Q is a very early document which predates or ignores the Jesus movement's campaign to turn Jesus into the Messiah and the Son of God.

Like the Gospel of Mark, Q starts off with John the Baptist and has no tales of a baby Jesus or a resurrected Jesus.

The Gospel of Matthew

The Gospel of Matthew is a blend of the Gospel of Mark, "Q" (see above), and some material that is distinctive to Matthew which academics have labeled "M".

This Gospel repeats about 90% of what is in Mark.

This Gospel is very concerned to portray Jesus as Jewish and often jumps in with quotes from the Old Testament to prove how Jesus is the fulfillment of Israelite scriptures. This indicates that this Gospel was originally written with a Jewish readership in mind.

The Gospel of Matthew aims to portray Jesus as a second Moses who has come with a new covenant and to rescue the Jews by sacrificing himself. A few of the parallels Matthew creates:

1. The Pharaoh slaughtered all the Israelite boys, with only Moses being saved (Exodus Chapters 1-2). Likewise, Matthew has Herod kill all the male babies in Bethlehem with only Jesus being saved (Matt 2:13-18).

2. The great journey of Moses is to come out of Egypt, leading the Israelites. Likewise, Matthew has the baby Jesus spirited away to Egypt so that he too can later come out of Egypt. (Matt 2:13-21).

3. Moses brings down the Ten Commandments from a mountain. Likewise, Jesus proclaims the Beatitudes on a mountain (Matt 5:1).

4. The first five books of the Hebrew Bible (Genesis, Exodus, Leviticus, Numbers, Deuteronomy) are attributed to the authorship of Moses. Likewise, Matthew has Jesus give five major discourses (Matt 5-7, 10, 13, 18, 22-25). This causes the author to mash together things that were almost certainly said at different times.

The writer is also determined to prove that Jesus is the foretold Jewish Messiah. In order to make this case, he doesn't hesitate to radically embellish passages from the Gospel of Mark. Mark 8:29 reads:

> And he asked them, "But who do you say that I am?" Peter answered him, "You are the Messiah."

In the Gospel of Mark, Jesus does not reply to Peter's claim. But the writer of the Gospel of Matthew transubstantiates this simple Markan passage into divine proof that Jesus is the Messiah and the Son of God and that, moreover, Peter would become the legitimate head of the burgeoning first-century Jesus movement:

> He said to them, "But who do you say that I am?" Simon Peter replied, "You are the Messiah, the Son of the living God." And Jesus answered him, "Blessed are you, Simon Bar-Jonah! For flesh and blood has not revealed this to you, but my Father who is in heaven. And I tell you, you are Peter, and on this rock I will build my church, and the gates of hell shall not prevail against it. I will give you the keys of the kingdom of heaven, and whatever

> you bind on earth shall be bound in heaven, and whatever you loose on earth shall be loosed in heaven." (Matt 16:15-19)

In a gymnastic feat of double-think, in order to make his case that Jesus had the genetic credentials to be the second Moses and the Messiah, Matthew commences his Gospel with a family tree starting off with Abraham, proceeding through King David and ending up with Joseph then Jesus (Matt 1:1-16)… and then he immediately proceeds to say that Jesus was not the son of Joseph but was a son of the Holy Spirit (Matt:1:18-21).

The Gospel of Luke

Luke (1:1-4) starts off his Gospel specifically admitting that he is creating a composite Gospel based on previous writings:

> Many have undertaken to draw up an account of the things that have been fulfilled among us, just as they were handed down to us by those who from the first were eyewitnesses and servants of the word. With this in mind, since I myself have carefully investigated everything from the beginning, I too decided to write an orderly account for you, most excellent Theophilus, so that you may know the certainty of the things you have been taught.

Luke's Gospel is a blend of the Gospel of Mark, Q, and material distinctive to this Gospel referred to by scholars as "L".

Luke reproduces about 50% of the Gospel of Mark.

Luke's story has a more universal feel. He seems to be writing with both a Jewish and Gentile readership in mind. Accordingly, he deletes the Markan episode most likely to cause offense to Gentiles: the story of the Gentile woman who comes to Jesus to beg for help for her possessed daughter (Mark 7:24-30).

Like Matthew, Luke has a nativity story at the beginning (though a completely different one) and resurrection material at the back end.

Like Matthew, Luke had access to a far more pristine version of the Gospel of Mark than we do. As such, it is possible that some of the Markan material found in Luke is actually truer to the original version of Mark than extant versions of the Gospel of Mark. For instance, the earliest known versions of the Gospel of Luke record Jesus's baptism by the Holy Spirit in this way:

> "And it so happened, when all the people were baptized, and after Jesus had been baptized and while he was praying, that the sky opened up, and the holy spirit came down on him in bodily form like a dove, and a voice came from the sky, "You are my son, today I have become your father."
>
> - Luke 3:21-22. Translation from Robert J. Miller (ed), *The Complete Gospels*.

There is no reason why Luke would have altered a passage in Mark in this direction so, just possibly, it is more like the original Markan passage than the version of Mark that we now have:

> And a voice came from heaven, "You are my beloved Son; with you I am well pleased."
>
> - Mark 1:9-11

Later versions of Luke were altered by scribes to make that passage more doctrinally correct, so now Bibles generally record the words in Luke as: "You are my beloved Son; with you I am well pleased."

The other big difference in this account of the baptism is that, in Luke, there is a noticeable time gap: first there is Jesus's baptism in water, and only later does the Holy Spirit descend while Jesus is praying. (See Appendix One.)

The Gospel of John

The Gospel of John is out-there different to the first three Gospels. The Gospel of John is based on a very different tradition. It hints that it owes its authority to "the disciple whom Jesus loved the most" (John??).

The whole thrust of the Gospel of John is to prove that Jesus was the Son of God and it frankly admits to this bias:

> Now Jesus did many other signs in the presence of
> the disciples, which are not written in this book;
> but these are written so that you may believe that
> Jesus is the Christ, the Son of God, and that by
> believing you may have life in his name.
>
> - John 20:30-31

There is a very strong anti-Jewish sentiment in this Gospel. The Jews are the ones totally to blame for the crucifixion of Jesus. Their fault lay in their not recognizing that Jesus was the Son of God and so they committed deicide – killing their own God. This indicates that this Gospel was written with an exclusively Gentile audience in mind.

To give you an idea of how out-there different the Gospel of John is, we only need to consider the phrase "the kingdom of God" – which is what the Jesus of the Synoptic Gospels said his ministry was all about. The phrases "the kingdom of God" or "kingdom of heaven" are mentioned 14 times in Mark, 36 times in Matthew, and 32 times in Luke – noting that Matthew and Luke are both far longer than Mark. That same phrase – "the kingdom of God" – appears a grand total of two times in the entire Gospel of John.

It is very hard to reconcile the earthy preacher in the Gospel of Mark who uses parables with the wordy lecturer in the Gospel of John who uses no parables. The Johannine Jesus seems to talk about himself for an inordinate amount of time. Things that Jesus **may** have said privately to his disciples are wrapped into extremely long discourses. Obviously, these cannot be verbatim accounts.

My opinion is that the Gospel of John probably contains some things that Jesus said privately to his disciples but these have been coalesced, expanded upon, and supplemented in order to form diatribes.

In trying to understand what the historical Jesus was actually like, you have to make a choice between the Jesus in the Gospel of Mark and the Jesus in the Gospel of John. The general academic consensus is that the Gospel of John is extraordinarily problematic as a guide to the life and character of the historical Jesus. In line with this, I only cite a few passages from the Gospel of John.

The Christian Church through the ages has largely gone with the Jesus of the Gospel of John.

The Letters of the Apostle Paul (50 to 58 AD)

If you read the epistles of Paul after reading the Gospels, you tend to think, "Why didn't he cite the words of Jesus more?"

It needs to be realized that Paul never read any of the Gospels because he was writing before they were widely available.

Scholarly experts now consider that only seven epistles in the New Testament can reliably be attributed to Paul. In probable chronological order, they are:

1. First letter to the Thessalonians
2. Letter to the Galatians
3. Letter to the Philippians
4. Letter to Philemon
5. First Letter to the Corinthians
6. Second Letter to the Corinthians
7. Letter to the Romans

If you want to get a handle on understanding Paul, read these seven letters in the above order.

Of the other epistles traditionally ascribed to Paul:

- Colossians and Ephesians are considered to be written by students of Paul with a good grasp of his ideas.
- The second letter to the Thessalonians is considered to be an inept rewriting of an original Pauline letter.
- The letter to Titus and both letters to Timothy are considered to be clearly not by Paul.

See Garry Wills, *What Paul Meant* pp.15-16.

Non-biblical Sources: The Nag Hammadi Library

In December 1945, an astounding discovery was made near Nag Hammadi in Egypt. Locals digging for fertilizer accidentally uncovered a sealed earthenware jar containing thirteen leather-bound papyrus books and some pages torn from another book. These books had been sealed up for centuries. It is theorized that they were hidden there in the fourth century because of an official church clampdown on "heretical" Christian texts.

The texts were written in Coptic, this being the language of Egypt at that time. It is likely that they were all translations from Greek.

Some of these books are "early Christian Gnostic" texts with elaborate stories about creation and angels, etc, etc. They are painful to read and not much use for shedding light on the life of Jesus or anything else. Not to put too fine a point on it: they are junk. But there are a few extremely noteworthy exceptions.

The Gospel of Thomas (date in dispute)

There were existing fragments of the Gospel of Thomas in Greek but finding a full version in Coptic at Nag Hammadi was the pearl beyond price.

It seems to have been the most revered of the Nag Hammadi texts as it was written on the best-quality papyrus.

It is a "sayings Gospel" – being a collection of 114 sayings attributed to Jesus.

I have used the Thomas O. Lambdin translation from James M. Robinson (ed), *The Nag Hammadi Library*.

The dating of this Gospel is tricky because it is a collection of sayings and, as such, is more vulnerable to having more sayings added to it with the passing of years. I would argue for a very early date, not many years after the death of Jesus.

(For more on dating this Gospel, see the Wikipedia article on the Gospel of Thomas.)

The Gospel of Philip (any time from 150 to 350 AD)

Not much of a "Gospel" in the sense that it has nothing on Jesus's life and very few sayings that are even attributed to him but it is pure gold as the reflections and observations of a Christian mystic or, more likely, a number of Christian mystics.

The title "Gospel of Philip" is actually a modern attribution. The text doesn't have a title and happens to mention the disciple Philip.

Both the Patterson Brown and the Wesley W. Isenberg (WI) translations can be found at http://gospelofthomas.nazirene.org/philip.htm. I mainly use the Patterson Brown translation. When I use the Isenberg translation, I specify this by "WI" but I still reference the numbering of the Paterson Brown translation.

The Gospel of Mary (second century or late first century – some scholars date it even earlier than this)

The contents of this gospel tie in with the idea that Jesus gave secret teachings to his disciples. This gospel intimates that the disciple whom Jesus loved the most was Mary.

Significant slabs of it are missing but it definitely gives the impression that the proper Christian path is one of inner spiritual growth.

I have used the translation in James M. Robinson (ed), *The Nag Hammadi Library* pp. 293-296.

Non-biblical Sources: Other

Josephus, *Antiquities of the Jews* (93-94 AD)

Josephus was an Israelite army officer in the Jewish-Roman War of 66-73 AD. He managed to make a timely extraction of himself from the routed Jewish forces, dodged a suicide pact, and transferred his allegiance to Rome. He ended up living in Rome where, in the last quarter of the 1st Century, he wrote a number of works about the Jews. These have become crucial to the understanding of Jewish life in that era. His writings include *Antiquities of the Jews* in which he mentions both John the Baptist and Jesus.

One of his two mentions of Jesus is generally accepted as genuine. It is about the stoning of James, "the brother of Jesus, who was called Christ" (Antiquities 20:9.1). The other mention is generally considered to have been significantly doctored by some later Christian true believer. See the Wikipedia article, "Josephus on Jesus".

Josephus's passage on John the Baptist is considered genuine:

> Now some of the Jews thought that the destruction of Herod's army came from God, and that very justly, as a punishment of what he did against John, that was called the Baptist: for Herod slew him, who was a good man, and commanded the Jews to exercise virtue, both as to righteousness towards one another, and piety towards God, and so to come to baptism; for that

the washing [with water] would be acceptable to him, if they made use of it, not in order to the putting away [or the remission] of some sins [only], but for the purification of the body; supposing still that the soul was thoroughly purified beforehand by righteousness. Now when [many] others came in crowds about him, for they were very greatly moved [or pleased] by hearing his words, Herod, who feared lest the great influence John had over the people might put it into his power and inclination to raise a rebellion, (for they seemed ready to do any thing he should advise,) thought it best, by putting him to death, to prevent any mischief he might cause, and not bring himself into difficulties, by sparing a man who might make him repent of it when it would be too late. Accordingly he was sent a prisoner, out of Herod's suspicious temper, to Macherus, the castle I before mentioned, and was there put to death. Now the Jews had an opinion that the destruction of this army was sent as a punishment upon Herod, and a mark of God's displeasure to him. (Flavius Josephus, *Jewish Antiquities* 18. 5. 2. Translation by William Whiston).

The Gospel of the Hebrews (early 2nd Century)

Regrettably, only small fragments of the Gospel of the Hebrews survive in critiques of it by early Church Fathers such as Jerome and Origen. See Robert J. Miller (ed), *The Complete Gospels*, pp. 425-434.

The Upanishads and other mystic writings

I have also drawn on the writings of mystics from Christian and other traditions. See the Select Bibliography.

My Source

In the beginning and in the end, there is one seminal reason I ended up writing this book: the inner work I have done and the experiences that came from that. In 1991, I had a series of unanticipated experiences which set me on a path – a very winding path – which led to the writing of this book. Without those experiences, no book.

If you are interested to know more about my inner journey:

renlexander.com   **youtube.com/@drrenlexander.**

Appendix Three

Timeline of Jesus[46]

Major event	Comment	Best guess
Birth of Jesus		5 BC
Jesus baptized in water by John the Baptist	Mark 1:9 Around the age of 29 (Luke 3:23)	24 AD
Stays in the wilderness as a disciple of John the Baptist	Considering deep spiritual transformation is not done overnight, Jesus likely stayed in the wilderness with John for a couple of years.	24-26 AD
Baptism by the Holy Spirit	Mark 1:10-11	26 AD
Gap between Jesus's baptism by the Holy Spirit and arrest of John the Baptist	Looking at the Biblical accounts, it would seem that Jesus was not with John when he was arrested. Once baptism-by-Spirit had taken place, he likely did not stay in the wilderness with John. It is possible Jesus went back to construction work. (Mark 1:14).	27 AD

---

[46] There is a very clear and concise discussion of issues to do with estimating a timeline for Jesus at Wikipedia, "Chronology of Jesus".

John the Baptist is arrested	Mark 1:14	28 AD
Jesus starts to gather disciples and preach	Immediately after Jesus learns that John has been arrested (Mark 1:14-15).	28 AD
Starts to wander the towns and villages preaching	Mark 1:14 – Mark 10	28 AD
Jesus sends out the Twelve to preach to greater Israel	Mark 6:7-13	29 AD
John the Baptist sends enquiry to Jesus "Are you the one who is to be next?"	Luke 7:18-23	Late 29 AD
John the Baptist is beheaded	Mark 6:14-29	Early 30 AD
The turning point: Jesus suddenly announces that he must suffer and die	Seemingly only a short time after the beheading of John the Baptist (Mark 8:31).	Early 30 AD
First mention of an apocalyptic "Son of Man"	Immediately after Jesus announces that he has to suffer and die (Mark 8:62 – Mark 9:1).	

Transfiguration	Six days later (Mark 9:2-3).	30 AD
Jesus sets out for Jerusalem	Shortly after Transfiguration, Jesus sets out for Jerusalem, timing his journey so that he will arrive there shortly before Passover (Mark 9-10).	30 AD
Entry into Jerusalem	Around a week before the day of the Passover (Mark 11:1-11). Passover happens on the 15th day of the Jewish month of Nisan. In the year of 30 AD, this was in April.	Late March or early April 30 AD
Trashing the temple	The next day (Mark 11:12-19).	30 AD
Preaching in Jerusalem	The days after trashing the Temple (Mark 11:20 – 12:44).	30 AD
Long apocalyptic diatribe to four disciples	Shortly before Passover (Mark:13)	
The Last Supper	Evening of the first day of the Passover (Mark 14:12-25). Thursday evening. Jewish days last from dusk to dusk. The Passover lasts seven days.	April 6th 30 AD

Arrest in Gethsemane	A few hours after the Last Supper (Mark 14:43-51). Thursday night.	30 AD
Crucifixion	The day after being arrested. First day of the Passover. (Mark 15:20-41).	Friday April 7th 30 AD
Sabbath	Nothing could happen on the Sabbath. If Jesus was in a tomb, no-one could go and tend to his body. Friday evening until Saturday evening.	Saturday April 8th 30 AD
Sightings of dead Jesus commence	The first sighting reported is as being on Sunday, the day after the Sabbath. (1 Corinthians 15:3-8; Luke 24; Matthew 28; John 20-21).	Sunday April 9th 30 AD
Last sighting of Jesus (Paul and his conversion experience)	Paul spent time persecuting Jewish members of the growing Jesus movement so there would surely have been at least a couple of years before his conversion experience occurred (1 Corinthians 15:8).	Not before 32 AD

<u>Appendix Four</u>

The Quest of the Apocalyptic Jesus

Amongst present-day academic Biblical historians, the received position is that Jesus was an apocalypticist: he was preaching an upcoming upheaval of Armageddon proportions which would lead to the establishment of a "kingdom of God" on Earth. Under this interpretation, the "kingdom of God" is an external earthly kingdom that will be established by an apocalyptic event. This makes Jesus's entire life and ministry a miserable failure because the apocalypse never came. It makes Jesus into a deluded and irrational man – not a great spiritual teacher at all.

Though not original to him, this apocalyptic view of Jesus was established as the academic standard in 1906 by Albert Schweitzer in *The Quest of the Historical Jesus*. Brilliant as his book was, Schweitzer's eschatological view of Jesus is ultimately based on a fundamental misunderstanding of the phrase "the kingdom of God". Once you take away that mistaken understanding, the vast majority of the evidence for Jesus being an apocalyptic preacher evaporates.

But not all.

Only a handful of days before his arrest and crucifixion, Jesus would sit down with just four of his disciples:

> And as he sat on the Mount of Olives opposite the temple, Peter and James and John and Andrew asked him privately, "Tell us, when will these things be, and what will be the sign when all these things are about to be accomplished?" And Jesus began to say to them, "See that no one leads you astray. Many will come in my name, saying, "I am he!" and they will lead many astray. And when you hear of wars and rumours of wars, do not be alarmed. This must take place, but the end is not yet. For nation will rise against nation, and kingdom against kingdom. There will be earthquakes in various places; there will be

famines. These are but the beginning of the birth pains.

"But be on your guard. For they will deliver you over to councils, and you will be beaten in synagogues, and you will stand before governors and kings for my sake, to bear witness before them. And the gospel must first be proclaimed to all nations. And when they bring you to trial and deliver you over, do not be anxious beforehand what you are to say, but say whatever is given you in that hour, for it is not you who speak, but the Holy Spirit. And brother will deliver brother over to death, and the father his child, and children will rise against parents and have them put to death. And you will be hated by all for my name's sake. But the one who endures to the end will be saved.

"But when you see the abomination of desolation standing where he ought not to be (let the reader understand), then let those who are in Judea flee to the mountains. Let the one who is on the housetop not go down, nor enter his house, to take anything out, and let the one who is in the field not turn back to take his cloak. And alas for women who are pregnant and for those who are nursing infants in those days! Pray that it may not happen in winter. For in those days there will be such tribulation as has not been from the beginning of the creation that God created until now, and never will be. And if the Lord had not cut short the days, no human being would be saved. But for the sake of the elect, whom he chose, he shortened the days. And then if anyone says to you, "Look, here is the Christ!" or "Look, there he is!" do not believe it. For false christs and false prophets will arise and perform signs and wonders, to lead astray, if possible, the elect. But be on guard; I have told you all things beforehand.

"But in those days, after that tribulation, the sun will be darkened, and the moon will not give its light, and the stars will be falling from heaven, and the powers in the heavens will be shaken. And then they will see the Son of Man coming in clouds with great power and glory. And then he will send out the angels and gather his elect from the four winds, from the ends of the earth to the ends of heaven.

"From the fig tree learn its lesson: as soon as its branch becomes tender and puts out its leaves, you know that summer is near. So also, when you see these things taking place, you know that he is near, at the very gates. Truly, I say to you, this generation will not pass away until all these things take place. Heaven and earth will pass away, but my words will not pass away.

"But concerning that day or that hour, no one knows, not even the angels in heaven, nor the Son, but only the Father. Be on guard, keep awake. For you do not know when the time will come. It is like a man going on a journey, when he leaves home and puts his servants in charge, each with his work, and commands the doorkeeper to stay awake. Therefore stay awake—for you do not know when the master of the house will come, in the evening, or at midnight, or when the rooster crows, or in the morning— lest he come suddenly and find you asleep. And what I say to you I say to all: Stay awake."

- Mark 13:3-37

This is by far the longest monologue ascribed to Jesus in the Gospel of Mark. In the English translation, it contains 685 words. How do you think you would go at recalling this speech verbatim if you were one of the four disciples listening to it?

You just read it. How much can you recall?

It is certainly understandable that the disciples and others would recall pithy sayings by Jesus: "Blessed are the poor in spirit for theirs is the kingdom of heaven." And one can also understand that people would recall the parables. These are short stories and images – easy to recall. Moreover, Jesus would have doubtlessly repeated these a number of times. Even your average Western atheist will be able to recall a couple of Jesus's parables such as, for instance, The Good Samaritan.

But a 685-word rant said just once to just four people? What are the chances that it is flawlessly remembered and recalled?

Non-existent.

Almost certainly, the author of the Gospel of Mark has vastly inflated anything apocalyptic which Jesus might have said. There were two factors likely to cause such an exaggeration:

1. He was writing in the heyday of the belief in the imminent apocalyptic Second Coming of Jesus;
2. Apocalyptic passages in the Book of Daniel which twice mention "the son of man" (Daniel 7:13 and 8:17). In Daniel, the expression "son of man" really only means "person" but it was enough for early Christians to make a connection with Jesus's use of "the Son of Man" and connect it with apocalyptic passages in Daniel. Indeed, in Matthew's version of this apocalyptic rant, he references the Book of Daniel: "So when you see the abomination of desolation spoken of by the prophet Daniel, standing in the holy place (let the reader understand), then let those who are in Judea flee to the mountains." (Matt 24:15-16).

Even allowing that Mark gave himself a huge degree of license, certainly Jesus could well have said something apocalyptic privately to four disciples. But that, in itself, means that Jesus was *not* primarily a preacher of a forthcoming apocalypse. He *only* shared this vision with *four* people *in private* towards the end of his life. Take away the wrongful apocalyptic decoding of "the kingdom of God" and it means he was not primarily a preacher of an apocalypse to the general public. If he really was an apocalyptic preacher, shouldn't this private talk have been the public talk he was giving? Not obscure talk of a "kingdom of God" and mustard seeds and yeast but instead a full-on boots-and-all Technicolor imaging of the apocalypse. If he was primarily a preacher of the apocalypse then this is the talk he should have and would have been giving from the very beginning. Certainly that is the sort of talk given by modern apocalyptic preachers.

There is an also a long diatribe in Luke and Matthew which clearly reads apocalyptically. Again, it is made after the Transfiguration and, again, it is only said in private to his disciples.

And he said to the disciples, "The days are coming when you will desire to see one of the days of the Son of Man, and you will not see it. And they will say to you, "Look, there!" or "Look, here!" Do not go out or follow them. For as the lightning flashes and lights up the sky from one side to the other, so will the Son of Man be in his day. But first he must suffer many things and be rejected by this generation. Just as it was in the days of Noah, so will it be in the days of the Son of Man. They were eating and drinking and marrying and being given in marriage, until the day when Noah entered the ark, and the flood came and destroyed them all. Likewise, just as it was in the days of Lot – they were eating and drinking, buying and selling, planting and building, but on the day when Lot went out from Sodom, fire and sulfur rained from heaven and destroyed them all–so will it be on the day when the Son of Man is revealed. On that day, let the one who is on the housetop, with his goods in the house, not come down to take them away, and likewise let the one who is in the field not turn back. Remember Lot's wife. Whoever seeks to preserve his life will lose it, but whoever loses his life will keep it. I tell you, in that night there will be two in one bed. One will be taken and the other left. There will be two women grinding together. One will be taken and the other left."

- Luke 17:22-36 (See also Matt 24:36-44)

This one is a mere 279 words.

Again, we have to ask why, if Jesus was primarily an apocalyptic preacher, this isn't the talk that he was giving to everyone and not just to his disciples?

It's not like it is hard to understand.

If he was an apocalyptic preacher, why didn't he eschew the obscure parables and just let loose with these talks instead?

Do you notice anything missing from these two apocalyptic passages?

Have a glance back over them... something that definitely and absolutely would have to be there if Jesus was primarily a preacher of a forthcoming Apocalypse?

?

There is absolutely no mention of "the kingdom of God".

Remember that this is what Jesus said his mission was: to preach the kingdom of God.

If Jesus's concept of the coming of the kingdom of God was inextricably enmeshed in a belief in a forthcoming Apocalypse then these diatribes are *exactly* where he would use the phrase "the kingdom of God".

There would be phrases like:

- "And this is how the kingdom of God will be established on Earth"
- "And this presages the coming of the kingdom of God on Earth"
- "After this, the kingdom of God will be founded."

Nothing.

Not even a hint of a mention of "the kingdom of God".

The pivotal thesis of *The Jesus Code* is that "the kingdom of God" references a mystical possibility for the soul. These two passages show no evidence of a direct link between Jesus's concept of a forthcoming Apocalypse with his concept of "the kingdom of God".

Let us look at another apocalyptic passage – one that actually does make use of the word "kingdom". Again, this speech is only given to the disciples in private and not the general public:

> "Just as the weeds are gathered and burned with fire, so will it be at the end of the age. The Son of Man will send his angels, and they will gather out of his kingdom all causes of sin and all law-breakers, and throw them into the fiery furnace. In that place there will be weeping and gnashing of teeth. Then the righteous will shine like the sun in

the kingdom of their Father. He who has ears, let him hear."

- Matthew 13:40-42.

Tellingly, even though this speech mentions a "kingdom", it does NOT mention "the kingdom of heaven" or "the kingdom of God". It mentions instead "the kingdom of their Father" – the only time this phrase appears in the Bible.

"You are those who have stayed with me in my trials, and I assign to you, as my Father assigned to me, a kingdom, that you may eat and drink at my table in my kingdom and sit on thrones judging the twelve tribes of Israel. (Luke 22:28-30)

This passage, thought to be an excerpt from Q, is vastly toned down in the Gospel of Matthew (so much so one wonders if these two passages had a joint origin in Q):

Jesus said to them, "Truly, I say to you, in the new world, when the Son of Man will sit on his glorious throne, you who have followed me will also sit on twelve thrones, judging the twelve tribes of Israel (Matt 19:28).

The passage from Luke is seems to be a popular citing among academics seeking to substantiate the view that Jesus was a failed apocalyptic prophet yet it is actually a very anomalous passage. It is the only time the phrase "my kingdom" appears in the synoptic Gospels. As the author of Matthew isn't shy about pushing Jesus's credentials, this passage looks to have had a mammoth embellishment in the Gospel of Luke. In any case, it does not mention the "the kingdom of God" and any "judging" that is to take place could be on a spiritual rather than an earthly plane.

It is hard to know how Jesus could have done more to separate out the idea of "the kingdom of God" from the aftermath of the Apocalypse. Academics have just assumed that apocalyptic passages refer to the establishment of "the kingdom of God" on Earth – despite the total absence of that phrase in apocalyptic passages.

With a proper understanding of the expression "the kingdom of

God", we can reject the idea that Jesus was primarily an apocalyptic preacher.

In Part I: The Turning Point, we saw that Jesus did come to suddenly talk about a forthcoming apocalyptic reckoning of souls to be led by "the Son of Man". Such talk only started a handful of weeks before his crucifixion. In the months or even years of his ministry prior to that, he never says anything about a Son-of-Man-led apocalypse. Moreover, even in his last weeks, he didn't preach an apocalypse to the masses but, apart from one possible mention to the general public (Mark 8:38), he only said these things in private to his disciples. (See discussion of this in Part I).

Plainly, Jesus was not primarily a preacher of a forthcoming apocalypse.

The quest for the historical Jesus has reached its endpoint. He was not a delusional apocalyptic preacher who happened to teach some spiritual things. He was a spiritual teacher who, as a result of his journey, came to arrive at a belief in a forthcoming apocalyptic reckoning of souls to be led by "the Son of Man".

Appendix Five

Something on nothing

Separated by centuries, mystics independently claimed that everything started with "Being".

Not nothing.

Being… Beingness… Isness…

They came to this conclusion because when they purified their soul, their experience was not of nothing; it was of Being.

But, I hear you cry: *"Surely before Being was, there must have been nothing."*

It turns out, there is no such thing as nothing.

If I ask you to picture this "nothing", chances are you will think of black space. If I ask you where one might find a piece of this "nothing", you will likely reply: "Out in space, between stars."

If I ask you to describe what happens in this piece of nothing in space, you would almost certainly say: "Nothing".

Modern science absolutely and irrevocably disagrees with you. Quantum mechanics has shown that all "empty" space is seething with activity – matter and anti-matter are popping in and out of existence in the void.

Einstein's Theory of General Relativity demonstrated that the supposed nothingness of space actually interacts with solid objects. Objects bend the void of space-time. In turn, the bent void of space guides the motion of objects. Arguably, the void – the "nothing" – has density. It must have density for it to be bent.

Remember when I asked you to picture nothing and you pictured a black empty space? But isn't "space" a something? Get rid of that space and really truly visualize nothing. Perhaps you may now visualize a black point. Perhaps even that black point disappears, and you are left now with what? Perhaps you now visualize a white space – a white space devoid of black. But isn't that space a something?

We can visualize a space devoid of white. We can visualize a space devoid of black. But we cannot visualize or imagine a no-thing.

We can not think. But we cannot think of "Nothing".

Nowhere is there or has there ever been "nothing".

The idea of "nothing" was only ever a theory which has now been disproven by science. Of course, we can have an absence of particular things: no cows, no planets, no stars. But we cannot have an absence of everything.

The *idea* of nothing exists (as much as an idea can be said to exist): the idea exists that nothing is an absence of everything. But without things, you couldn't have even the idea of the absence of every thing. Even the idea of nothing is dependent on things.

Some readers may now be freaking out*: "No really, there MUST have been nothing before there was any sort of something!"*

Take a deep breath.

What you are saying is "Nothing must have existed before there was something that existed".

Nothing cannot exist.

Only things with Being can exist.

Some readers will be freaking out more than ever: *"No! Truly! Really! Before there was something… before there was even this "Being" stuff… there MUST have been NOTHING!"*

To which I would simply reply…

Why?

Why must have there been this mysterious non-existent "nothing" stuff before there was Being? Why? "Nothing" is a much more mysterious concept than "Being".

There is and never has been nothing.

Nowhere is there nothing.

Nothing is nowhere.

The truth is that if there was really "nothing" at the very beginning then that is all there ever would have been.

There would have never ever been a some thing.

The mystics were right.

In the beginning was Being.

An historical implication

The following is an extract from a forthcoming book, *The Journey of the Souls and the Meaning of Life*. I have included it here as an appendix because this same issue – the attachment of souls to ape bodies – arises in this book.

An historical implication: A sudden discontinuity

Broadly speaking, religions have never even begun to come to terms with Darwin's theory of evolution by means of natural selection. Its advent was an intellectual earthquake that shook Christianity to its philosophical knees. The challenge posed by Darwinian evolution was that it dispensed with the need for a divine creator to explain the wondrous diversity and patterns amidst life on Earth. It also contradicted the account of creation in the Bible.

Accepting Darwinian evolution as true raises a question for Christians, people of all faiths and spiritual people generally: *When during evolution did creatures start to have souls? As single-celled organisms? At fish level? At primate level? When?*

The Journey of the Souls does not touch the question of whether other animals have some sort of souls but it is very specific about "human souls". Human souls are special: derived from a divine "spawning". They would be rejected by God and come to attach themselves to "ape" bodies. These initial attachments to physical bodies would not just be events in amorphous "divine" time but events in earthly archaeological time.

There is a startling implication from this: that the sudden attachment of human souls to ape bodies would impact on the behavior of the species they attached themselves to. We would expect that there would be a discontinuity – that there would be a change in behavior of the chosen species which could not be attributed to any physical evolutionary change.

Is there any evidence for a sudden discontinuity in human cultural evolution? That suddenly our ancestors turned in a completely different direction?

Actually – and this may well shock a lot of readers – there is a stunning amount of evidence for it.

It even surprises me that the evidence is so very great.

For many years I was aware that the Journey of the Souls implied that there would be a historical discontinuity but I supposed that any discontinuity would be so long ago that there wouldn't be any real evidence for it. It was only in 2010 that I took an interest in archaeology and realized that this implication of the Journey of the Souls was right – that there is a massive historical discontinuity in the behavior of one particular species – *Homo sapiens*.

It is sometimes referred to by archaeologists as "The Great Leap Forward".

The species known as *Homo sapiens* originally evolved around 200,000 years ago. For as much as 150,000 years nothing happened. For all those millennia, Homo sapiens showed only marginal more promise than other ape species. Their basic tool was a sharpened stone which hadn't evolved for millennia – our ancestors hadn't even thought to attach a piece of wood to it. This was our one claim to fame – we carried around a rock. Also we doubtless carried around sharpened sticks. Even this wasn't even much of a claim to fame: we weren't even the only species using tools. Some birds use twigs to get at something they want.

"Homo sapiens" means "wise man" or "knowing man". For as much as 150,000 years our species was not even remotely worthy of that name. It would have been more appropriate to refer to us as "*Homo insapiens*" – "unknowing man".

Then, in the blink of an archaeological eye, everything changed – and it changed without any physical or genetic alteration on the part of the species.

Around 50,000 years to 75,000 years ago, our species made a giant leap from being rock-carrying apes into displaying what is referred to as "behavioral modernity":

- Art appeared in cave paintings and figurines
- Beauty became an issue with the use of pigments and jewelry
- Music appeared
- Games started to be played

- The level of tool-making jumped dramatically
- Food was cooked and seasoned instead of eaten raw
- Living space became organized instead of resembling the randomness of a pack of animals
- Barter and exchange between groups started to flourish
- We became bolder explorers and pushed into new areas like Australasia and Northern East Asia
- Most startling of all: we stopped simply abandoning our dead and started to bury them – indicating a belief in an afterlife. Gifts were even buried with the deceased.

There is no evolutionary explanation for this: our bodies and brains and genes were *exactly the same* but, quite suddenly, *everything changed*. It was a giant leap forward with no genetic explanation.[47]

But there is an explanation in terms of the Journey of the Souls – this huge discontinuity marks the point in time at which human souls began attaching themselves to "ape" bodies and so human beings were created. We ceased to be the species *Homo insapiens* and became *Homo sapiens*. Fifty thousand years ago, *Homo sapiens* was born. It was born by the attachment of human souls to the bodies of *Homo insapiens*.

When we think about giant leaps in human thought, we are inclined to think of great scientific theories like Darwin's Theory of Evolution, Einsteinian relativity, Newtonian mechanics or the Periodic Table of Elements but there is no leap in human thought that is as large and inexplicable as a tribe of apes suddenly deciding that there was life after death. Only because this particular belief has been around for so very long do we fail to appreciate what a titanic leap it was. For 150 millennia, a species has absolutely no belief in life after death then suddenly it does.

How could this happen?

Indeed, arguably, the entire edifice of all knowledge and science is built on this one gigantic insight: that there is more to the world and

---

[47] Some archaeologist believe they can date the start of the Giant Leap as long ago as 75,000 BC. Whatever the actual exact date, there seems no getting around the fact that for over a hundred thousand years, nothing happened and then, for no genetic reason, the behavior of Homo sapiens was completely transformed. It seems that human souls also tried incarnating into Neanderthals and Cro-Magnons as evidenced by artwork.

life than we can immediately see with our physical eyes and immediately touch with our physical hands.

And it was this belief that was somehow born at the time of the Giant Leap.

One of the strongest indicators of the Giant Leap is the advent of cave art. For a long time, the popular theory was that cave paintings identified animals that the primitives wanted to successfully hunt. This theory left a large number of questions unanswered – including why they would paint them in caves – indeed, sometimes paint them in the most inaccessible parts of the cave.

It is now thought that cave art were depictions of "spirit quests" and experiences from trances. Far from depictions of the external world, they were depictions of an internal world.

What was born in the Giant Leap was not an instant greater mastery of the outer world. What was born was an inner world: an inner world that appreciated beauty and neatness and music and taste and the fun of games and could imagine new tools and life after death.

Without one shred of genetic change.

The Great Leap was so extraordinary that it has been characterized as "the big bang of human consciousness".

To try to get a handle on how extraordinary it was, imagine that gorillas suddenly started doing this – painting cave art, showing evidence that they believed in life after death, playing music, making tools. We would be gob-smacked. This would be like Planet-of-the-Apes-type stunning.

It is no less stunning that *Homo insapiens* started doing it.

This period of the Great Leap looks to be the identifiable period where human souls began to attach themselves to "ape" bodies. Indeed, this "incarnation" of the "human" souls is the only viable explanation for a cataclysmic change in species behavior *that has no physical basis*.

Such a radical change in the behavior of an entire species without any genetic change simply does not fit in with the theory of evolution by means of natural selection.

Because the theory of evolution by means of natural selection has itself evolved since Darwin's brilliant *Origin of Species*, it is actually hard to find a definitive statement of the theory of evolution. I am going to attempt one here.

The modern theory of evolution by means of natural selection:

- The behavior of any species is determined or circumscribed by its genes.
- Individual organisms in species throw up genetic variations.
- If the genetic variation affects the behavior or health of the organism, it can have a positive or negative impact on its survival and breeding.
- If the effect of the new gene is beneficial in that environment, it will be preferentially selected. Over time, more and more offspring will come to possess that gene. The species as a whole will change/evolve.

Can an entire species radically change its behavior without any shred of genetic change? Absolutely not. At least not under the theory of evolution.

However, the attachment of "human" souls to *Homo insapiens* does yield an explanation of a change which cannot be made sense of under the theory of evolution.

Doubtless many archaeologists and others who consider themselves scientific atheists will be aghast at this idea and desperately galvanized into the search for an alternative explanation.

One likely counter-argument will be something to do with "memes" – a meme is an idea that gets a life of its own and is passed on from person to person, generation to generation. This alternative explanation will be something like: 50,000 years ago, a mad genius invented the idea of life-after-death and it went viral.

But the truth is that, prior to this big bang of human consciousness, nothing worthy of the name "meme" even existed. It is in this period of the Great Leap where ideas worthy of the designation "meme" were born. Oh yes, some animals could do basic imitation. Lyrebirds can imitate the call of other birds. Is that a meme? Monkeys can imitate behavior of other monkeys. Early *Homo insapiens* could copy the other early humans in the making of sharp rocks. I suppose we could stretch the concept and call such imitations "proto-memes" but they were nothing like the sophisticated memes that were born during this period of the big bang of human consciousness.

For what was born in this period was not just "memes" but – really remarkably – a hunger for "memes': for ideas, for new experiences.

Consider the bizarre advent of neatness – of keeping one's living space in order. For millennia, *Homo insapiens* lived like pack animals. Does it seem remotely likely that some genius started tidying up their living space and suddenly members of the same tribe and other tribes saw it and said, "Gee, I really want to keep up with the Joneses and tidy up my living space"?

It is incredibly unlikely unless there was an underlying psychic shift in the species as a whole.

Another implication of this period of discontinuity is that there would have been a period of overlap – a time when there lived both some Homo sapiens with human souls and some Homo insapiens without human souls. The "human" Homo sapiens would have interacted with and bred with Homo insapiens.

I have zero interest in arguing in favor of *The Book of Genesis* nevertheless, fascinatingly, that book makes an allowance for such an overlap. In *Genesis*, the first two humans, Adam and Eve, gave birth to Cain and Abel. In Chapter 4, Cain slew Abel, fled and "settled in the land of Nod, east of Eden... had relations with his wife and she conceived, and gave birth to Enoch."

In light of the Journey of the Souls, that does sound like a portrayal of human-souled Homo sapiens breeding with genetically identical Homo insapiens.

There is another implication for some world religions that is worth mentioning. Some religions portray an "infinitely reincarnating" soul: before we were incarnated into the bodies of hairless apes, we were incarnated in dogs, in birds, whatever. What would have been impressive is if the relevant religious figures had, through awareness of their past lives, predicted the existence of dinosaurs or other extinct animals on the basis of recalling pre-human incarnations. As far as I know, none ever did. The Journey of the Souls portrayed in this book does not posit "infinite reincarnation" through all manner of species. It posits a point of time where human souls started to attach themselves to ape Homo insapiens bodies... and so, it would seem, dovetails in with archaeological evidence.

Finally, let me note this: it is considered one of the greatest pieces of confirmation for a scientific theory that it makes an unlikely prediction – a prediction completely unlikely except in terms of the theory – and this unlikely prediction turns out to be correct. This is exactly what the Journey of the Souls did: it made a completely unlikely prediction that our ancestors totally changed their behavior without one shred of genetic change. How unlikely is that under the theory of Darwinian evolution by means of natural selection?

Can not happen.

Under Darwinism, radical changes in a species' behavior can only happen with a genetic change which is preferentially selected.

Yet the prediction of the Journey of the Souls turns out to be correct: the behavior of our ancestors radically changed without one shred of genetic change.

If unexpected-but-confirmed prediction is good enough as a test of the truth of a scientific theory, it is good enough for the test of the truth of a spiritual theory.

And so it is that spirituality and the theory of evolution by means of natural selection are reconciled.

Acknowledgments

I am humbled by my debt of gratitude to so many people living and dead... every mystic whom I have quoted in this book... Carl Jung... the author of the Gospel of Mark... the author (or authors) of the Gospel of Philip... the author of the Gospel of Matthew for preserving the Beatitudes.

Ahrara Bhakti, without you, quite possibly no book.

Karen Daniels... thank you.

Pamela Matthews, my rock and fellow soul-traveler, with whom I swapped inner work sessions for 14 years.

Laurence Harrould who very kindly read an early version of the manuscript and patiently attempted to convey the essence and history of the spiritual path of his race and religion. His thoughtful input has, I hope, resulted in a more empathetic rendering of the Israelite religion up to the time of Jesus.

The teachers of the classes I did at the then Universal Christian Gnostic Movement. They helped me make greater sense of my inner journey. Unfortunately, they also told me that I couldn't have had that journey because it wasn't done using their techniques so I had to leave their classes... but I didn't leave my gratitude behind.

And so many of the authors of the books in the Bibliography. In particular, I would like to make a respectful nod to Bart D. Ehrman who has produced so many works based around the received academic view on Jesus: that Jesus was preaching the coming of an imminent apocalypse (the coming of "the kingdom of God"). I have benefited greatly from the clarity of his writings and lectures.

Select Bibliography

Almaas, A.H., *Essence. The Diamond Approach to Inner Realization,* (Red Wheel Weiser: 1986).

Armstrong, Karen, *A History of God. The 4000-Year Quest of Judaism, Christianity and Islam* (Ballantine Books: New York, 1993).

> *Fields of Blood: Religion and the History of Violence* (Alfred A. Knopf: 2014)

Aslan, Reza, *Zealot. The Life and Times of Jesus of Nazareth* (Random House: New York, 2013).

Besant, Annie, *Esoteric Christianity* (Theosophical Society: 1905; 2nd edition)

Easwaran, E., (transl), *The Upanishads* (Nilgiri Press: Tomales, California, 1987).

Eckhart, Meister, *Eckhart: A Modern Translation,* translated by Raymond B. Blakney (HarperTorch: 1986).

> *Selected Writings,* translated by Oliver Davies (Penguin, 1994).

> *The Complete Mystical Works of Meister Eckhart,* translated and edited by Maurice O'C Walshe (The Crossroads Publishing Company: New York, 2009).

Ehrman, Bart D., *The Orthodox Corruption of Scripture. The Effect of Early Christological Controversies on the Text of the New Testament* (Oxford University Press: New York, 1993).

> *Jesus. Apocalyptic Prophet of the New Millennium* (Oxford University Press: 1999).

> *Lost Christianities: The Battles for Scripture and the Faiths We Never Knew* (Oxford University Press: 2003).

> *Misquoting Jesus: The story behind who changed the Bible and why* (HarperSanFrancisco: 2005).

> *The Lost Gospel of Judas Iscariot* (Oxford University Press: 2006).

> *Peter, Paul and Mary Magdalene: The Followers of Jesus in History and Legend* (Oxford University Press: 2008).

Jesus, Interrupted. Revealing the Hidden Contradictions in the Bible (and Why We Don't Know About Them) (HarperCollins eBooks: 2009).

Forged: Writing in the Name of God – Why the Bible's Authors Are Not Who We Think They Are (HarperCollins: 2011).

Did Jesus Exist? The Historical Argument for Jesus of Nazareth (HarperOne: 2012)

How Jesus Became God: The Exaltation of a Jewish Preacher from Galilee (HarperOne: 2014).

James, William, *The Varieties of Religious Experience: A Study in Human Nature* (Longmans, Green & Co: 1902).

Jung, C.G., *Aion. Researches into the Phenomenology of the Self*, translated by R.F.C. Hull (2nd edition; Princeton University Press: Princeton, 1968).

Answer to Job, translated by R.F.C. Hull (2nd edition; Princeton University Press: Princeton, 1969).

Levine, Amy-Jill, Dale C. Allison Jr and John Dominic Crossan (ed.), *The Historical Jesus in Context* (Princeton University Press: Princeton, 2006).

Miller, R.J. (ed), *The Complete Gospels. Annotated Scholars Version* (Revised and expanded edition; HarperSanFrancisco: San Francisco, 1994).

O'Reilly, Bill, and Martin Dugard, *Killing Jesus. A History* (Macmillan 2013).

Plotinus *The Enneads* as translated in W.R. Inge, *The Philosophy of Plotinus* (3rd Edition; Longmans, Green & Co: New York: 1929).

Robinson, James M. (ed), *The Nag Hammadi Library* (HarperCollins: 1981).

Schweitzer, Albert, *The Quest of the Historical Jesus* (1906). You can download it for free from gutenberg.org. There is also a free, very good talking book version at.librivox.com.

St John of the Cross, *The Collected Works of Saint John of the Cross*, translated by Kieran Kavanaugh & Otilio Rodriguez

(Revised edition; Institute of Carmelite Studies: Washington, 1991).

St Teresa Avila, *The Interior Castle* (Christian Classics Ethereal Library). Available for free at ccel.org. The section of the most interest is the last one, "The Seventh Mansions".

Stace, W.T., (ed) *The Teachings of the Mystics* (Mentor Books: New York, 1960).

Steiner, Rudolf, *Christianity as Mystical Fact* (1902).

  Approaching the Mystery of Golgotha (1914).

  Autobiography: The Story of My Life (1928).

  Free talking book versions available at rudolfsteineraudio.com.

Wills, Garry, *What Jesus Meant* (Viking Penguin: 2006).

  What Paul Meant (Viking Penguin: 2007).

  What the Gospels Meant (Viking Penguin: 2008).

Online resources:

biblehub.com Excellent website - particularly useful for checking comparative translations.

biblestudytools.com Excellent search engine. Very useful for checking such things as word usage frequency.

ccel.com Christian Classics Ethereal Library. Many free out-of-copyright resources. Impressive collection.

earlychristianwritings.com A very wide range of early Christian literature for free.

gutenberg.org Thousands of free out-of-copyright books. For instance, Albert Schweitzer's *The Quest of the Historical Jesus*.

librivox.org Out-of-copyright talking books.

<u>wikipedia.com</u> A wonderful starting resource for any subject to do with
Biblical studies.

You can also purchase university-level courses on Bible studies, Jewish history and Christian history from <u>thegreatcourses.com</u>. These are done by top-level academics. Highly recommended..

The Crucifixion Code and The Jesus Code are part of The Meaning of Life series

Dr Ren Lexander's **The Meaning of Life** series is the most comprehensive and complete look at the question of the meaning of life in history. It covers psychology, spirituality, philosophy and much more. It presents the final answer to the questions:

- What is the meaning of life?

- And how then can I create an ultimately meaningful life?

The most important series of books you will ever read.

What is the meaning of life?

This is a question that concerns each and every one of us in the most piercing and dramatic way possible – for in the answer to this question lies the path to a truly meaningful life for each one of us."

This book examines common ideas about the meaning of life – ideas that have shaped individual lives and shaped the history of our planet: ideas such as "life is about preparation for the hereafter", "life is about the pursuit of pleasure" and "life is meaningless".

We shall see that, in the end, there are only two rational answers to the question of "What is the meaning of life?"

And one of these is that life is meaningless…

"Life begins on the other side of despair."

– Jean-Paul Sartre

Without question, one of the most important books you will ever read.

This book explains how a confrontation with meaninglessness (despair, depression, etc.) can lead to a new and better you... and a new and more meaningful life.

If you yourself are currently going through depression, despair, disillusionment, this is the book you most need to read.

Should you know someone who is in a confrontation with meaninglessness, this is the book they most need to receive.

WARNING!

"For many readers, reading this book will be one of the most confronting experiences of their lives. Prior to starting to read it, please have a source of psychological and/or emotional support lined up – whether this be a professional therapist or just someone you can talk to. I do not recommend that you read this book with a partner as the danger is that at least one of you will start trying to talk the other one out of reading it (as a way of talking themselves out of reading it."

The Journey of the Souls

and

the
Meaning
of
Life

Ren Lexander

Part of The Meaning of Life series

The ultimate answer to the question:
What is the meaning of life?

Well… it would be a great shame if all this contemplation of the single biggest question of all time didn't lead to a few jokes, stories and whimsical observations…

Stay up-to-date with releases at renlexander.com